Shield of Protection

Katherine E. Schmidtke

**Doctor of Biblical Studies
in Biblical Counseling**

PRESS

Contents

Preface

As a phone counselor for TBN ministries, I got a call from a woman evangelist who wanted me to join her in prayer for a good, healthy husband. The one she had was in prison and she had divorced and remarried him several times. She had two sons who died from overdosing on drugs. Her 20 year old granddaughter was pregnant, trying to get out of an abusive relationship. The grandmother was on Social Security Income because of a spinal problem.

The same day I got a call from a young man who was depressed. His live in girlfriend left him and he was in pain. And, yes, they had been intimate with each other.

The next call came from a divorced mother who was having trouble with her teenage son who was truant from school again. She couldn't handle him any more and the boy's father who lived in California was not available to take him at this time. The mother was dating another man and her son was very disrespectful and unmanageable when the boyfriend came over.

All three of these calls represent the story of how the enemy tries to kill, steal and destroy God's children.

How is it that Ezra, his family and leaders of the Jewish community, could take a journey from Babylon to Jerusalem, through marauding territory and not be damaged, while others taking the same road, were captured, robbed, bloodied and many died before they reached their destination?

Believers today are on a journey to reach their goal and can expect the same kind of protection that Ezra and his group received as they traveled to Jerusalem.. It would be beneficial for Christians to figure out what Ezra did to receive special protection from God.

Here is Ezra's story. <u>Ezra 8:21-23,31-32</u> "Then I declared a fast while we were at the Ahava River so that we would humble ourselves before our God; and we prayed that he would give us a good journey and protect us, our children, and our goods as we traveled. For I was ashamed to ask the king for soldiers and cavalry to accompany us and protect us from the enemies along the way. After all, we had told the king that our God would protect all those who worshiped him, and that disaster could come only to those who had forsaken him! So we fasted and begged God to take care of us. And he did.

"We broke camp at the Ahava River at the end of March

and started off to Jerusalem; and God protected us and saved us from enemies and bandits along the way. So at last we arrived safely at Jerusalem."

This book relates how we as Christians disregard spiritual laws and unknowingly puncture our shield of protection to permit the fiery darts of Satan to enter into our space; thus causing deep wounds, sickness, depression and hopelessness. It reveals how to recognize the root causes and how to repair the damage.

Chapter 1
Read All About It

It is time for the 'born again' Christian to take his/her place in the Kingdom of God and enjoy the 'shield of protection' that Jesus Christ bestows upon every believer. What is the Shield of Protection? It is a spiritual, veiled, protective covering that is around the followers of Christ. In the Bible it is described in different ways: as a protective hedge, shield, blood of the Lamb, shadow, angels, mother hen, and others.

Most of us are knowledgeable about physical laws of nature because our parents have taught or trained us or we break those laws to discover the consequences. The law of gravity can't be seen, but it certainly becomes obvious if we break this law. If someone decided to walk off a ten-story building, the law of gravity would become quite obvious to the person falling through space to his death.

Spiritual laws are not so obvious because the average

Christian is not made aware of the consequences when they occur even though they are as deadly as falling off of a ten-story building. A story that socks even Christians is the story of Ananias and Sapphira that comes out of Acts 5:1-11. Here was a couple that thought they could lie to the Holy Spirit about a promise they had made to Peter concerning property they had sold. They lied about the full price they received. Peter said, 'How could you and your husband even think of doing a thing like this— conspiring together to test the Spirit of God's ability to know what is going on? Just outside that door are the young men who buried your husband, and they will carry you out too.' Instantly she fell dead." (TLB)

Lying to the Spirit of God — that is something that is done every day and people don't drop dead. The question is: does the spirit of death enter or do we break the shield or hedge of protection and let death enter?

This writing project will cover how to keep your shield of protection up because when the 'hedge comes down the snake comes in.' Ecc. 19:8B KJV God our Heavenly Father wants to protect us from harm. We must be willing to be trained. Just as loving parents train and disciple their children about the physical laws in order to protect them from harm, Christian pastors, parents and teachers must be willing to teach the Bible's spiritual laws to believers.

Chapter 2

Protective Covering Revealed

When a person is Born Again, he is born out of the kingdom of Satan's world and born into the Kingdom of God - Heaven - Jesus. We don't disappear from this earth but we are now citizens of heaven. (Col 3:3 TLB) As a matter of fact, we mingle with people who are either in one kingdom or the other. However, in the Kingdom of Jesus there is a covering of protection around the believer that the fiery darts of Satan can't penetrate.

Illustration # 1 of the two kingdoms.

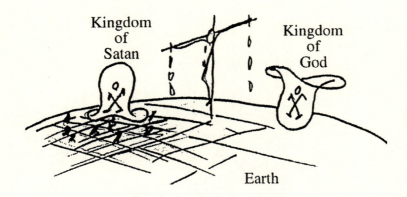

Let's take a look at this protective covering through the experience of Job. In the story of Job we see that God put a hedge of protection around him. As a result of that hedge, the blessings of peace, prosperity, health and well being were evident in his family. Satan, on his own, could not penetrate the protective covering that God put upon him. We see the picture in Job 1:9-10, Satan replied to God. "Does Job fear God for nothing? Have you not put a hedge around him and his household and everything he has? You have blessed the work of his hands, so that his flocks and herds are spread throughout the land." (NIV)

Job's story lets the Christian know there is a protective covering. The godly person can count on the shield of protection covering his family, just as Job experienced God's security. When the protective hedge was lifted from Job, he lost his children, his likelihood and his health. What went wrong? The problem is exposed in the first chapter and corrected in the last chapter of Job. He feared God and stayed away from Evil. It was also his practice to rise up early in the morning and make a burnt offering for his sons just in case they had sinned and had cursed God in their heart. (Job 1:1,5) This religious activity was evidence that Job knew about God.

In the last chapter of Job he has a remarkable change (42:5-6) "But now I say, 'I had heard about you before, (first chapter) but now I have seen you, (last chapter) and I loathe myself and repent in dust and ashes.'"(TLB)

The distinction between knowing about God and seeing Him makes all the difference to God. When a person encounters the Lord, as Job did, his religion changes to a personal relationship which was apparently what God wanted from Job because in Job 42:10 "the Lord restored Job's wealth and happiness! In fact, the Lord gave him twice as much as before!" (Job 42:12) "So the Lord blessed Job at the end of his life more than at the beginning. Then at last he died, an old, old man, after living a long, good life."(TLB)

A person who meets God face to face as Job experienced, will not venture far from His presence.

Job is not the only example in the Bible that illustrates God's protective covering.

> Ps 5:12. For you bless the godly man, O Lord; you protect him with your <u>shield</u> of love. <u>Ps 7:10</u> God is my <u>shield</u>; he will defend me. He saves those whose hearts and lives are true and right. <u>Ps 28:7</u>. He is my

strength, my <u>shield</u> from every danger. I
trusted in him, and he helped me. (TLB)

Though we may or may not see angels around us, they
are there to guard His children. Tom tells the story of running lickety split home at the dinner call of his mother. As a
seven-year-old he was not attentive of the truck rolling down
the street. The truck and he should have collided, but something pulled him back from certain death. His mother was
confident it was his guardian angel.

> <u>Ps 91:11-13</u> "For he orders his angels to pro-
> tect you wherever you go. They will steady
> you with their hands to keep you from stum-
> bling against the rocks on the trail. <u>Matt
> 18:10</u> "Beware that you don't look down
> upon a single one of these little children. For
> I tell you that in heaven their angels have
> constant access to my Father." (TLB)

Another type of protection coming from the Lord is the
blood covering available to the believer. Every time we par-
ticipate in communion, it is a reminder of the story found in
Exodus.

> <u>Exod. 12:23</u> "When the LORD goes through
> the land to strike down the Egyptians, he will
> see the blood on the top and sides of the door-

frame and will pass over that doorway, and he will not permit the destroyer to enter your houses and strike you down." (NIV)

What a comfort to know that the plagues that are rampant in our society today like AIDS, cancer and sexually transmitted diseases should not be touching the true believer's home or family if they are following His spiritual laws.

The blood of Jesus is sprinkled on the sinner who comes with a repentant heart to receive cleansing from all unrighteousness. This is a continual sprinkling for sin that may have slipped in. A believer will be convicted in his heart when something is amiss and needs to be repented of quickly when discovered. Roots of bitterness, anger and resentment cause a lot of problems in the believer's life even to the point of breaking his/her shield of protection.

Oral Roberts told a story about a mother hen who was found dead after the barn burnt down. The next morning the farmer and his wife found the hen all charred and nothing but dust. The farmer took the pitchfork to bury the remains and discovered, as he lifted the mother hen up, four little chicks under her burnt body alive and well. Not one little chick was harmed. Jesus tells the story of how he is likened to a mother hen.

Luke 13:34 "O Jerusalem, Jerusalem, you who kill the prophets and stone those sent to you, how often I have longed to gather your children together, as a hen gathers her chicks under her wings, but you were not willing!" (NIV)

What is it that we need protection from? Why aren't we able to do it on our own? There is but one answer and that is found in John 10:10: "The thief's purpose is to steal, kill and destroy." The thief in this case is Satan and we need protection from him and his cohorts.

Chapter 3

Big Problem

Now that we know that God wants and does provide protection for all of His children, why aren't all of His children experiencing this protection? The truth of scripture indicates that we are not all children of God and therefore don't fall under His protection and those that are His children are perishing for lack of knowledge.

Some Christians believe that we are all children of God just because we are God's creation. And Jesus' death on the cross meant that He died for the sins of the whole world, therefore we are all children of God and will go to Heaven. Scripture doesn't support this philosophy.

That Jesus died for the sins of the whole world is correct, but many of the world's children refuse to receive the good news of the Gospel and, as a result, do not receive the right to be called children of God but are known as children of Satan, of darkness, and of this world.

The problem started when Adam chose to disobey God's warning not to eat from the Tree of Conscience. Gen. 2:16b "for its fruit will open your eyes to make you aware of right and wrong, good and bad. If you eat its fruit, you will be doomed to die."(TLB)

Adam was given the credit for causing the dilemma that humans found themselves in throughout the ages. Rom. 5:17 "The sin of this one man, Adam, caused death to be king over all, but all who will take God's gift of forgiveness and acquittal are kings of life because of this one man, Jesus Christ." (TLB) Taking God's gift of salvation is an action that a sinner must take in order to receive Jesus and be cleansed of the Adamic sin nature that each person is born with.

The eye opener that describes what is transpiring on this earth happened at the confrontation that Satan had with Jesus during His forty-day wilderness experience.

> Luke 4:5-8 Then Satan took him up and revealed to him all the kingdoms of the world in a moment of time, and the devil told him, "I will give you all these splendid kingdoms and their glory— for they are mine to give to anyone I wish— if you will only get down on your knees and worship me." Jesus replied, "We must worship God, and him alone. So it is written in the Scriptures." (TLB)

Wake up! Wake up folks. If Satan is king over all the

kingdoms of this world, we can understand why we need to get into the kingdom of God. In Matt 6:33, Jesus states, "But seek first the kingdom of God and my righteousness, and all these things shall be added to you." (NKJ) When we are born again into Jesus' Kingdom, we become children of God.

Here's where the trouble unfolds. Matthew, Mark, Luke and John were written basically for the purpose of sharing the story of Jesus about his life, birth, death and resurrection. From that point on the rest of the Bible was written to the Church or the born again believers for the purpose of explaining, teaching and training the church body and believers. Children of God are those who have received the message of the Gospel and have been born out of the kingdom of darkness and born into the Kingdom of God by the transforming power of the Holy Spirit. (Col 1:13-14.) The believer is to read the rest of the Bible after being born again. The foundation comes first (Gospels), then the building blocks follow (the rest of the Bible).

Foundation: John 3:3: "Jesus replied, 'With all the earnestness I possess I tell you this: Unless you are born again, you can never get into the Kingdom of God.' John 3:8 Just as you can hear the wind but can't tell where it comes from or where it will go next, so it is with the Spirit. We do not know on whom he will next bestow this life from heaven."(TLB)

Building blocks (meant for the believers): Gal 3:26 "For now we are all children of God through faith in Jesus Christ," Phil 2:15. "You are to live clean, innocent lives as children of God in a dark world full of people who are crooked and stubborn. Shine out among them like beacon lights," I Jn 4:6 "But we are children of God; that is why only those who have walked and talked with God will listen to us. Others won't." (TLB)

Who are the others? The scripture characterizes them as heathens.

> Matt 5:47. "If you are friendly only to your friends, how are you different from anyone else? Even the heathen do that." Matt 6:31 "So don't worry at all about having enough food and clothing. Why be like the heathen?" Matt 20:25 "But Jesus called them together and said, 'Among the heathen, kings are tyrants and each minor official lords it over those beneath him.'" Acts 7:51 "You stiff-necked heathen! Must you forever resist the Holy Spirit?" 1 Cor. 5:1 "Everyone is talking about the terrible thing that has happened there among you, something so evil that even the heathen don't do it." (TLB)

These two different kingdom folks walk, work, live side by side on this earth. The Kingdom of God kids are not always aware that they have inherited a shield of protection, blessings of peace, prosperity, health and well being for their families, from the Lord.

Chapter 4

Broken Shield

As Christians we ought to be asking ourselves why are so many believers sick, depressed, addicted, fearful, suicidal, angry, broken, rebellious, not tithing, unequally yoked, living together outside of marriage, divorcing and living with no real joy, peace, prosperity, health or well being for their families. Quite frankly, there is something missing in their lives. Timothy communicates perfectly what is going on today.

2 Tim 3:1-5 "But mark this: There will be terrible times in the last days. People will be lovers of themselves, lovers of money, boastful, proud, abusive, disobedient to their parents, ungrateful, unholy, without love, unforgiving, slanderous, without self-control, brutal, not lovers of the good, treacherous,

> rash, conceited, lovers of pleasure rather than
> lovers of God– having a form of godliness
> but denying its power. Have nothing to do
> with them." (NIV)

The key to these verses is in the last line -"having a form of godliness but denying its power." This is one of the problems that is weakening the Christian's shield. Charisma Magazine, November 2003 put out an article entitled, "Annual Convention Marks 'Defining Moment' for Assemblies of God" by Peter K. Johnson. "The Assemblies of God was raised up to be a Pentecostal church in practice and not just in doctrine," Thomas Trask, General Superintendent, told Charisma, referring to churches that soft-pedal the Pentecostal experience and the gifts of the Holy Spirit. "Either we will be a Spirit - filled movement, or we will become a monument." This statement was voiced over the concerns about the AG's tepid growth in the United States.

What is missing from the Assembly of God? According to Acts 1 and 2 it's the outpouring of the Holy Spirit.

> Acts 2:17-18 "In the last days,' God said, 'I
> will pour out my Holy Spirit upon all
> mankind, and your sons and daughters shall
> prophesy, and your young men shall see
> visions, and your old men dream dreams.
> Yes, the Holy Spirit shall come upon all my

servants, men and women alike, and they shall prophesy." (TLB)

The Holy Spirit brings to the person that is filled with the Holy Spirit nine fruit - to build up the persons character. Gal 5:22-23 "But when the Holy Spirit controls our lives he will produce this kind of fruit in us: love, joy, peace, patience, kindness, goodness, faithfulness, gentleness and self-control." (TLB) Christians who show just the opposite fruit ought to check out their relationship with the Holy Spirit.

The nine gifts of the Holy Spirit flow as the person goes out to minister. In 1 Cor. 12:8-10 you have the nine gifts listed as: word of knowledge, word of wisdom, discerning of spirits, gift of faith, gifts of healing, working of miracles, prophecy, gift of tongues, gift of interpretation of tongues. Keep in mind that all nine gifts flowed through Peter and Paul as they went out to minister, likewise when we go out to minister in the power and strength of the Holy Spirit the gifts will follow. A person who receives the Holy Spirit brings with him all nine fruit and all nine gifts.

When the Pentecostal story is taught, believed, received, and applied, people will be supernaturally empowered to live life with a purpose. My own grandsons received the Baptism in/with the Holy Spirit one evening on a weekend sleepover at my home. Just before bed time the seven-year-old wanted to show me how well he could read the Bible. He wanted me to pick out the selection. I chose Acts 1 and 2. All at once they both wanted to know more about the experience the disciples had in the upper room. I told them and we prayed for the same encounter. They started to speak in tongues immediately. At 3:00 a.m, I woke up hearing them whispering in their sleeping bags. Once they knew I was awake the oldest one reported that the Lord visited him and told him he would be a missionary for the Lord. At fifteen he has been on two missionary trips into South America, he is learning Spanish for a purpose, and his life is directional and not floundering. When the Holy Spirit comes in, supernatural things start to happen. God wants to equip His children with miracle working power that comes from the Holy Spirit. Elizabeth's story illustrates a life that was collapsing until she had a confrontation with the Lord:

I considered myself a Christian, being brought up in the Roman Catholic faith, but never had a close relationship with Jesus. At the age of thirty, everything in my life kept going down hill, my marriage ended, I left a good paying job, I lost money on whatever venture I tried, and I was sinking into a state of depression.

I left my country of Trinidad and came to the United States to start over. While praying one night, at about 4:00 a.m., I heard a knock at my window. Looking out from the third story, I saw a car stopped. As I lowered my eyes in the direction of the car lights, I saw the vilest thing. It was lost anguishing souls in Hell.

Then, my attention was drawn upward to see a magnificent lighted cross shining in the night sky. The valley of decision was set before me, to choose Jesus or the Devil. Tears flowed as I surrendered my life to Jesus. The very next Sunday I was in church where I felt at peace. Some friends invited me to attend a church where they taught Growth Classes. I was taught about the Holy Spirit and was gloriously filled and began to speak in tongues.

Around 3:00 a.m. I was awakened by a mournful, pitiful cry - incessant in my ear. It would not go away. I kept praying to the Lord to put that soul to rest. I was told to read Isaiah chapter 1.

I couldn't wait to share the news with my teacher. In describing this incident to her she made this comment. "Elizabeth, sometimes when we are young we do things that are not pleasing to the Lord." While she was talking, I immediately thought of the abortion I had a couple of years earlier which I choose to erase from my memory. She recommended we read together Isaiah 1:15 "From now on, when you pray with your hands stretched out to heaven, I won't look or listen. Even though you make many prayers, I will not hear, for your hands are those of murderers; they are covered with the blood of your innocent victims." (TLB) I became convinced that abortion is murder. When I repented something left my body and I have been delivered and set free.

In this testimony the Holy Spirit was the counselor that revealed the sin that was causing depression, migraine headaches, no joy, just plain darkness. The Holy Spirit and the word of God did the work eliminating the expense of counselors.

Christians carry with them what I call dead rats - hidden sins from the past, too painful to expose, but when the Holy Spirit does the work, the healing happens quickly. When the Holy Spirit is out of the picture, people get discouraged, hopeless and reflect to the community that God is not able to do miracles today.

Look at what is happening when the Pentecostal story is manifested in other parts of the World. The West used to be known as the center of Christendom, but there is evidence that Christendom has moved across to the Southern hemisphere of Asia. So says Dr. Phillip Jenkins of Pen State University, professor of History and Religious Studies and author of the book <u>The Next Christendom: Coming of Global Christianity</u>. He goes on to say that it is a Pentecostal, Spirit Filled movement that is sweeping the continents of Africa, Latin America and Asia. Dr. Jenkins reports that half of the population of Africa are believers. "There are more Pentecostals than Hindus" and "Christianity is growing faster than Islam and Buddhism." These believers are Bible centered, holding fast to the Old and New Testament.

Former <u>Time Magazine</u> correspondent, David Aikman, relates that there are more than 80 million followers in China and expected to capture 25 to 30% of that nation's people. Teams of evangelists are being sent to Scotland - home of the Presbyterians to Great Britain - Anglican roots, and to what was formerly the center of Christendom in the United States, for the purpose of re-evangelize the slumbering church.

With the accelerated growth of Christianity as a Pentecostal out pouring in Asia, India, and Africa, it is time for the Christians in America to rethink their attitude about the function of the Holy Spirit and his ability as our counselor, advocate, comforter, intercessor, helper and standby. To ignore his presence in our life, breaks down our shield of protection.

Another way to break our shield, individually and as a country, is to disregard the foundational truths that this country has historically built our country on.

Josh McDowell of "Josh McDowell Ministries," makes the statement, in his Video collection - <u>Beyond Belief to Conviction</u>, "The majority of our kids are simply not embracing the foundational truth of Christianity. They hold distorted beliefs and consequently they are being conformed to this world, rather than being transformed by the power of the living God."

"Those with distorted views are 200% more likely to physically hurt someone, 216% more likely to be resentful, 300% more likely to use illegal drugs and 600% more likely to attempt suicide."

He continues to point out the difference among youth between the actions of a Christian and non-Christian behavior on: " who cheated on a test? 74% Christian, 76% non-Christian; who lied to a teacher 83% to 85%, who lied to a parent 93%, 93%; who physically hurt someone when angered 63%, 67%; who was satisfied with their ethics and character 91% to 90%? Christianity, makes little or no difference in the lives of our young people."

Taking the Bible out of school, the influence of secular music, death, sex and war games symbolized in video games, abortion, and divorce has taken its toll on our youth. The moral foundation of today is based on situational ethics. Why are we surprised when two young men dressed in long black coats penetrated the Columbine High School building killing twelve students and one teacher before killing themselves?

People asked, "Why did God allow this to happen?" Let us not be so quick to blame God for what is happening today. From the book, "America: To Pray Or Not to Pray," by David Barton, the facts are: "As a result of Supreme Court decisions on June 25, 1962, and June 17, 1963, 39 million students were told they could no longer pray or read their Bibles in school." The following is the prayer that was struck down, "Almighty God, we acknowledge our dependence on thee and beg thy blessing over us, our parents, our teachers, and our nation Amen."

As a result of the Supreme Court's judgement the following are the documented results of that action on "us," "our parents," "our teachers"and "our nation" since 1963. The research started in 1952 and went to 1986. From 1952 to 1962 all of the statistics were fluctuating slightly. But in 1963 scores took off.

- ("Us") Teen pregnancies up 400%, Gonorrhea among 10- 14 year old up 1,000%, teen suicide up 300%, depression among youth up 1,000%, violent crime up 660%;
- ("Our parents") divorce up 120%, unmarried couples living together up 600%, single house holds 500%;
- ("Our teachers") SAT scores dropped 800%;
- ("Our nation") violent crime up 660%"

This is a picture of a biblical one-liner: "When the hedge of protection (prayer and Bible) comes down, the snake comes in."

The Supreme Court was not finished. In 1980 the ACLU presented before the court in the case of Stone V. Graham against having the Ten Commandments displayed in public schools. As a result of the ACLU winning, the Ten Commandments disappeared from our schools. Can we say that our schools have become safer as a result of removing the moral laws of our nation? I would say the exact opposite is true. There have been more killings, rapes, abuse, cruel hazing, drugs and disrespect for human life: not less.

Judge Moore has taken a stand for the display of the Ten Commandments in the court house, public parks, and government buildings where they have been representing our country for, in some cases, 50 to 100 years. (As of November 2003, he is out of office as a result of this stand.) Our very laws of this nation are built upon the moral laws of the Ten Commandments. The ACLU is coming against the foundation of our country. Was the shield of protection over our Nation penetrated on September 11, 2001 as a result of our foundation cracking?

> Luke 6:47-49 "But all those who come and listen and obey me are like a man who builds a house on a strong foundation laid upon the underlying rock. When the flood waters rise and break against the house, it stands firm, for it is strongly built. "But those who listen and don't obey are like a man who builds a house without a foundation. When the floods sweep down against that house, it crumbles into a heap of ruins.""(TLB)

The hedge of protection over our country may be crumbling. It is, however, the responsibility of the Christian community to humble themselves and pray and seek the Lord's face and turn from their wicked ways, then the Lord will hear from Heaven and come and heal our land. (2 Chron. 7:14)

The foundational truths of the Bible were cracked when Rev. Gene Robinson of the Episcopal church became a Bishop as an active homosexual, living with his partner for thirteen years. According to a report put out by CNN; Rev. Gene Robinson believes that Jesus "places love above law"and that we are "all children of God." I have already reported in Chapter 3 the fact that the Bible indicates there are heathen folk and there are children of God indicating that we are not all children of God. As far as leading a homosexual lifestyle; Acts 15 tells us to "abstain from sexual immorality." The Bible is very clear about the fate of those who continue in homosexual activities.

> Rom. 1:26-27. That is why God let go of them and let them do all these evil things, so that even their women turned against God's natural plan for them and indulged in sex sin with each other. And the men, instead of having normal sex relationships with women, burned with lust for each other, men doing shameful things with other men and, as a result, getting paid within their own souls with the penalty they so richly deserved. (TLB)
> 1 Cor. 6:9. Don't you know that those doing such things have no share in the Kingdom of God? Don't fool yourselves. Those who live immoral lives, who are idol worshipers, adulterers or homosexuals— will have no share in his Kingdom. (TLB)

If the church leaders are going to lead their flock astray by their distortion of scriptures, the church has become an apostate group. An apostate means a defector, unfaithful, heretic, atheist.

Christians are responsible for knowing what the Bible

says. A "lack of knowledge" will cause a person to perish. It is quite possible that John F. Kennedy's family ran into problems because of not knowing how to come against a family curse that was spoken over the grandfather 150 years before. In the book review, <u>A Family Cursed?</u>, by William F. Buckley, it seems, Joseph Kennedy, on his way to start a new life in the United States, was disturbed by the distracting noises coming from the Jewish passengers who were celebrating high holy days of Rosh Hashana. Rabbi Jacobson put a curse on Kennedy "damning him and all his male offspring to tragic fates."

It is quite remarkable when you consider President John. F. Kennedy was assassinated in Dallas, Texas in 1963; brother Robert Kennedy was shot in 1968; an older brother of the President died in a plane crash in 1944; and his sister was killed in a plane crash in 1948; Sister Rose was put in a home for the mentally disturbed, Edward Kennedy was involved in a car accident that plunged off Chappaquiddick Bridge, thus killing Mary Joe Kipechne; and JFK Junior died along with his wife and sister-in-law in a plane crash in 1999.

It would seem in this case that the hedge of protection was down. Being Irish Catholics was the heritage of the Kennedy family. It is quite possible that if Joseph Kennedy knew his Bible, the following scripture could have been claimed and his family saved. <u>Isa 54:17</u> "No weapon that is formed against thee shall prosper; and every tongue that shall rise against thee in judgment thou shalt condemn. This is the heritage of the servants of the LORD, and their righteousness is of me, saith the LORD." (KJV) What is needed to keep the shield up is a personal relationship with Jesus, not religious activity.

There is a generation curse talked about in the Bible to the third and four generations and many Christian's fall into the trap of believing they will get hit with some disease that came from the family. Deut 5:9c "and I will bring the curse of a father's sins upon even the third and fourth generation of the children of those who hate me"

For the person who lives in the kingdom of God the generational curse has been broken, but the person must know the word of God that counteracts the curse found in Deut. 5:9 and Num. 14:17. This is where Satan gets away with murder as I believe he did for the Kennedy family and it is simply a lack of knowledge.

My sister was sure I would get a goiter because she had one and so did my mother. I was able to share the scripture that debunked the family curse. It is found in Jer. 31:29-30 "The people shall no longer quote this proverb— 'Children pay for their fathers' sins.' For everyone shall die for his own sins'" – and Ezek. 18:19-20 "'What?' you ask. 'Doesn't the son pay for his father's sins?' No! For if the son does what is right and keeps my laws, he shall surely live. The one who sins is the one who dies. The son shall not be punished for his father's sins, nor the father for his son's." (TLB)

If we have been "born again" into the Kingdom of God,

we must claim our inheritance. The "lack of knowledge" about God's provision is allowing Satan to penetrate the shield of protection. The Bible is clear about the blessings the Christian inherits right here, at this time, and on this earth. We are to seek first the Kingdom of God and His righteousness then all these blessings will be added unto "you".

On November 13, 2003, Christian Broadcasting Network reported a family living in one of the worst fire storms in California's history. While 3,200 homes were damaged by fire, their new home stood alone, unscathed. The fire jumped their home, burned all the homes down the street, on the right and left, and across the street, leaving about a ten-foot free area around their lot. Why was this home randomly selected to be saved and not the others? Perhaps it was because this family has a personal relationship with Jesus, and lives according to His righteousness.

This brings up the biblical story of Sadrach, Meshach and Abedego who were thrown into the ovens because they worshiped God alone. Those who threw them in were burnt to a crisp, but the three who were thrown in came out without the smell of smoke on them. (Dan. 3:14)

Look what happens to the family when a believer doesn't understand that there are demonic forces afoot trying to destroy the family. Eph. 6:12 "For we wrestle not against flesh and blood, but against principalities, against powers, against the rulers of the darkness of this world, against spiritual wickedness in high places." (KJV)

According to the Bible marriage between a man and a

36

woman is God's idea; <u>Matt</u> <u>19:5-6</u> "and that a man should leave his father and mother, and be forever united to his wife. The two shall become one— no longer two, but one!" He wants them to raise up righteous children. This union has a built in hedge or shield of protection for the family, placed there by God for the purpose of "training up a child in the way he should go: and when he is old, he will not depart." PROV 22:6

What happens to the children when divorce enters the picture? Children of divorce have more, "difficulty in school, behavior problems, negative self-concepts, problems with peers, and trouble getting along with their parents." (Focus on the Family)

What happens to the shield of protection when divorce enters the picture? For the child it is like earthquake conditions every day, nonstop. This produces stress, depression, health problems, economic difficulties and new and unexpected responsibilities. To keep Satan's fiery darts from penetrating the family's protective shield, following God's direction is important.

In the case of divorce and remarriage the Bible does have specific information. Marriage between two Christians is "until death do us part," exception being for adultery. If a Christian has been married as a Christian, and then divorced on any grounds other than adultery, he or she may not be remarried but is to remain unmarried or else be reconciled to the other partner. (1 Cor. 7:11)

Widows are able to remarry. Why? Because the spouse

doesn't exist on this earth any longer. The author, Stephen Gola, of <u>Divorce; God's Heart</u>, has stepped over the line to define the Biblical meaning of 'widow'. According to Gola, "The Bible tells us that 'widows' are women who have been divorced or deserted, as well as, those whose husbands are dead." Divorced and deserters still remain to cause lots of pain and heartache. Wounds stay opened and exposed to the fiery darts of the enemy.

For several years I worked with a program called <u>Before You Divorce</u> and found that Christian couples can be very creative when it comes to keeping their family together while being apart. Peggy and Larry lived in separate homes across the street from each other. This was the compromise they came up with: the husband ate the dinner meal with the family, played with the kids until bed time, then usually left for his home. The husband was then responsible for his own housekeeping. They were an affectionate, loving couple, but had different ideas about who picks up after the other. One house was neat as a pin the other was disorganized. Pets became a problem for the wife and the husband would not give them up, so they worked it out with two separate quarters. All the closeness of a husband and wife are still amorous and connected. This works for them and the kids are not divided from their family.

Another couple who had been divorced for seven years came back to renew their wedding vows. A job in another state separated them and the wife refused to move from her great job. The husband couldn't find work in Washington.

Seven years later the husband was transferred back home. He started attending a church where he met his former wife at the "Before You Divorce" class and they fell in love all over again.

Clair was a Christian who believed that her husband would come back to her even though they were divorced and he had taken up with a younger woman. She was at every Full Gospel Businessmen's meetings joining together with others in prayer for her husband's return. It took two years before the miracle happened. The younger woman kicked him out. Someone from Full Gospel Businessmen invited him to a meeting in another state where he was dramatically saved. It took him a year before he got enough nerve to call on his former wife. They started to date. Reconciliation took place and they were married in a small chapel. This couple ministers together for "Marriage Savers."

God has a plan for those that are in marriages that are intolerable, like the story from 1Sam 25:3-39 of Nabal and his beautiful, very intelligent wife, Abigail. The man, who was a descendant of Caleb, was "uncouth, churlish, stubborn, ill-mannered, bad-tempered, and a drunkard." Abigail was a wife who tried to keep her husband from getting killed, by feeding the man of God and his troops. When she arrived home, she found that Nabal had thrown a big party. He was roaring drunk, so she didn't tell him anything about her meeting with David until the next morning. "By that time he was sober, and when his wife told him what had happened, he had a stroke and lay paralyzed for about ten days, then died, for the Lord killed him. When David heard that Nabal was dead, he said, 'Praise the Lord! Nabal has received his punishment for his sin.' Then David wasted no time in sending messengers to Abigail to ask her to become his wife." (TLB) The moral of the story is stay true to the Lord and he will take care of you.

With the worldwide encroachment of the HIV virus infecting 42 million people, 29 million living in Africa, is the Christian to be concerned? Absolutely! It is imperative that the followers of Christ keep their lifestyle kosher.

Chapter 5

Are We All Sinners?

Among Christians I hear the comment that "we are all sinners and fallen short of the Glory of God. It is impossible to live without sinning." One pastor indicated that he would like to meet the person who didn't sin in the parking lot. I am terribly bothered by that philosophy and wonder, "When does the blood of Jesus take affect? When does it work?" Why would Jesus say in 1 Pet. 1:16, "Be ye holy; for I am holy." If we are supposed to be sinning, why did Jesus heal a man in John 5:14 and turn around to tell him "sin no more, lest a worse thing come upon you?" What a waist of time to proclaim in 1 John 2:1 "My little children, these things write I unto you, that ye sin not." And then in Rom. 6:1-2 "What shall we say then? Shall we continue in sin, that grace may abound? God forbid!" Paul laid it on the line in 1 Cor. 15:34. "Awake to righteousness, and sin not; for some have not the knowledge of God:

I speak this to your shame." Before we become a Christian, we are sinners and fallen short, but when we become "born again" we come into the Glory of God.

If we think that it is not possible to live a holy life before the Lord, "because we are just human - don't you know," then we will find no reason to be holy and when that happens the activity of the Christian will be no different from the person of the world and we can be sure that a fiery dart from Satan will come in with some kind of sickness.

By working with faith-based organizations and delivering the message to "abstain from sex until marriage, be faithful to your partner or use condoms if abstinence and fidelity are not practiced," the Uganda government discovered that they experienced the greatest decline in HIV infections of any Nation. As of this date (9/29/03) the USA Congress is still debating whether to follow Uganda's approach. This information came from the Heritage Foundation "The White House Initiative to combat AIDS: Learning from Uganda."

With the right lifestyle, the Christian's broken shield can be restored. I Jn 3:9 "The person who has been born into God's family does not make a practice of sinning because now God's life is in him; so he can't keep on sinning, for this new life has been born into him and controls him— he has been born again."(TLB)

If God's life is in the Christian then their ought to be a noticeable change of lifestyle and if there is not - head for the altar and pray for God's help.

Chapter 6
And The Enemy Is?

When I began reading the Bible for myself and discovering that Jesus went around healing the sick, raising the dead and casting out demons the thought entered my mind: What good does it do to read the miracles of 2,000 years ago if Jesus is not doing the same today? The answer came when I read Hebrews 13:8, "Jesus Christ the same yesterday, and today, and forever."

As I grew closer to the Lord and started to respond to the Word of God, Jesus made a personal visit and healed me from the top of my head to the bottom of my feet. From that point on, He trained me in what I call the shield of protection and the obstacles that poke a hole in the shield to cause great damage.

The following are examples of how we open the door to allow the fiery darts of Satan to trip us up. 1 Pet. 5:8 "Be careful— watch out for attacks from Satan, your great enemy. He prowls around like a hungry, roaring lion, looking for some victim to tear apart."

Obstacle # 1 <u>Not Reading the Word</u>.

I heard a story about a young man who had blown his mind on drugs. As a last resort his mother took him to church in hopes that prayer and association with the young people's group would have a good affect on him. He hadn't spoken a word for a whole year and spent his time just staring off into space. At one of the meetings he was anointed with oil and prayed for. No visible signs of healing took place. The mother was forced into thinking about putting him away in a mental institution. One evening she felt pressed to read the Bible. She read for hours, on into the midnight hours, then early morning, nonstop, until she finished. The last sentence came, she put down the book when she heard the first words her son had spoken in a year – "Read it again, Mom," The Word of God was quick, powerful and sharper than any two-edged sword, piercing even to the dividing asunder of soul and spirit. This young man is now a preacher sharing the power behind the Word.

Obstacle # 2 <u>Refusing to Forgive</u>

Many of us expect God to heal us without thinking that there might be something we are doing or have done that is holding up God's flow of power. For instance, the Lord's prayer, which most people are familiar with has this little thought in Mat 6:12, 14-15 "and forgive us <u>our </u>sins, just as we have forgiven those who have sinned against us. Your heavenly Father will forgive you <u>if you forgive those who sin against you; but if you refuse to forgive them, he will not forgive you.</u>" According to this phrase we actually plug up the healing power of God to us. Therefore, there is no healing, no joy, no peace, no life, no prosperity and no love.

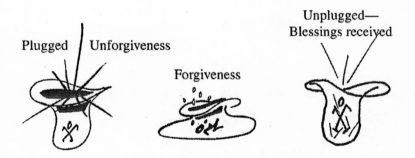

Plugged | Unforgiveness

Forgiveness

Unplugged—
Blessings received

Illustration: # 2 Forgiveness

A young woman discovered she had cancer of the throat. Doctors operated and determined there was no way of removing all of the cancer so they sewed her up and told her that she had three months to live. During the operation, the doctor cut the nerve to her left arm. In the meantime, the woman was attending a Bible centered church and getting excellent counseling for healing. God miraculously healed her of the cancer. Still, she was left having to take physical therapy to build up the strength in her deteriorating arm. She contacted a lawyer, having in mind that she would sue the doctor. At the same time she thought, "if God could heal me of the cancer he could heal me of the nerve damage" and decided to forgive the doctor. As she picked up the phone to cancel the lawsuit, feeling came back into her arm and she was totally healed. Thus, she demonstrated the spiritual law of forgiveness.

Obstacle #3 <u>Hidden Sin</u>

There is a story in the Bible about a man who had been sick for 38 years. Every day he laid by a pool that had a reputation of an angel ruffling the water and the first person in would be healed. Jesus spoke to the man and healed him. The interesting thing about this story is what happened the next day. Jesus went out of his way to find the man he had healed. In his conversation Jesus said, "Don't sin any more or a worse sickness will come upon you." Here is the significant part - Jesus indicated that this man had committed some kind of sin 38 years ago and it had bound him up for all 38 of those years. Not only that, but he was to stop it immediately. (John 5:2-15) It is interesting to know that the man Jesus healed was not too grateful, for he went immediately to find the Jewish leaders who had harangued him the day before, and told them "it was Jesus." The Jewish leaders were all the more eager to kill Jesus.

Unfortunately, just like this man who was healed, people enjoy their sin and don't like the idea of someone telling them to quit. To confront people with the rest of the story causes them to bristle at the very idea their sin caused the sickness. Nevertheless, sin punches a hole in our shield and the fiery darts of sickness and disease appears.

Chapter 7

Practicing Biblical–Scriptural Counseling

Jay E. Adams, who wrote the book <u>Competent To Counsel</u> would say that I am a Nouthetic Counselor which in my way of thinking is a Biblical - Scriptural Counselor.

The difference between a Humanistic (Worldly) Counselor and a **Nouthetic (Biblical Scriptural) Counselor** goes like this:

- Carl Rogers believes in a "non-directive" processes of therapy which entails responding back to the client what he said. **I am directive**.

- Abraham Maslow asserts man is basically good and has within himself all he needs. That may sound good, but is not what the Bible says. **I believe that we are all sinners in need of a Savior.**

- <u>Rollo May</u> theorizes that one thing is as good as the other - striving is useless so be content with who you are and what you have. **I believe that God has a plan for a persons life a plan for good and not for evil, and a person can be Born Again.**

- Fritz Perls affirms that conventional morals cut man off from freely experiencing life with his physical senses. If it feels good do it philosophy is his mantra. **I believe the Bible sets forth 'thou shalt not rules' to follow, overriding the feel good actions that may not be moral.**

- <u>Albert Ellis</u> believes a counselor is to be very directive in attacking certain unproductive behaviors of the client and tells the client what to do and how to think. **I believe that when a client is confronted with the Word of God there is a choice to be made. If his behavior is out of order, he should be isolated, reprimanded, or disciplined.**

It seems to me that **Jesus, God, the Holy Spirit, the Word of God, and the fellowship of Christians** are the superior counselors and my job is to lead people into their presence.

<u>Concerning Jesus</u>: "Come unto me, all ye that labour and are heavy laden, and I will give you rest. Take my yoke upon you, and learn of me; for I am meek and lowly in heart: and ye shall find rest unto your souls. For my yoke is easy, and my burden is light. Matt 11:28-30 Casting all your care upon him; for he careth for you." 1Peter 5:7

<u>Concerning God</u>: "If you will humble yourselves under the mighty hand of God, in his good time he will lift you up. Let him have all your worries and cares, for he is always thinking about you and watching everything that concerns you 1 Pet. 5:6-7 Fear not, for I am with you. Do not be dismayed. I am your God. I will strengthen you; I will help you; I will uphold you with my victorious right hand." Isa 41:10

<u>Concerning the Holy Spirit</u>: "May the grace of our Lord Jesus Christ be with you all. May God's love and the Holy Spirit's friendship be yours." 2Cor 13:14

<u>Concerning the Word</u>: "The whole Bible was given to us by inspiration from God and is useful to teach us what is true and to make us realize what is wrong in our lives; it straightens us out and helps us do what is right." 2 Tim 3:16

<u>Concerning Elders</u>: "Is anyone sick? He should call for the elders of the church and they should pray over him and pour a little oil upon him, calling on the Lord to heal him. And their prayer, if offered in faith, will heal him, for the Lord will make him well; and if his sickness was caused by some sin, the Lord will forgive him." James 5:14-15

I like what Biblical Discernment Ministries put out in the book, <u>How Christian Is Christian Counseling,</u> by Gary Almy. "The church is to rebuke, train, encourage, and gently disciple those who are troubled or are going astray." "To fail to do this, or to substitute human wisdom for God's revealed wisdom, is to fail to love." (Pg. 49-51)

I repeat, my job as a counselor is to lead people into the

presence of the Lord.

Some insights I have gleaned in thirty years of counseling folks who have "dis-ease" in their life will be uncovered in the next chapters.

Chapter 8

Mirrored Reflection

There are many stories in the Bible that promote the picture of mirrored reflection that I use in counseling. A "mirrored reflection" is a story or illustration or something you see that speaks to you as a revelation. My first recollection of a Biblical reflection came from Hosea 1:2, 2:2, 14, 18-20:

"Go and marry a girl who is a prostitute, so that some of her children will be born to you from other men. This will illustrate the way my people have been untrue to me, committing open adultery against me by worshiping other gods. I am no longer her husband. Beg her to stop her harlotry, to quit giving herself to others. But I will court her again and bring her into the wilderness, and I will speak to her tenderly there. "In that coming day," says the Lord, "she will call me 'My Husband' instead of 'My Master.' Then you will lie down in peace and safety, unafraid; and I will bind you to me forever with chains of righteousness and justice and love and mercy. I will betroth you to me in faithfulness and love, and you will really know me then as you never have before."

This is a story about Israel and how the people of God left him to get involved with other gods. God did not want to let them go. He went about wooing them back to him so they wouldn't ever want to leave Him because the door was opened to know him in a more personal way. The story is the mirror. One day I read it and realized this story was my story of what I had done. I saw my reflection in this story.

The story that Nathan told to David in 2 Sam 12:1-7, 13-14 is another type of "mirrored reflection." So the Lord sent the prophet Nathan to tell David this story: "There were two men in a certain city, one very rich, owning many flocks of sheep and herds of goats; and the other very poor, owning nothing but a little lamb he had managed to buy. It was his children's pet, and he fed it from his own plate and let it drink from his own cup; he cuddled it in his arms like a baby daughter." (**This touches the heart of David.**)

"Recently a guest arrived at the home of the rich man. But instead of killing a lamb from his own flocks for food for the traveler, he took the poor man's lamb and roasted it and served it." (**This was a crime.**)

"David was furious. "I swear by the living God," he vowed, "any man who would do a thing like that should be put to death; he shall repay four lambs to the poor man for the one he stole and for having no pity." (**David delivers the judgement.**)

Then Nathan said to David, "You are that rich man!" **(David sees himself in this story. His crime has been exposed - nothing is hidden)**

"I have sinned against the Lord," David confessed to Nathan. Then Nathan replied, "Yes, but the Lord has forgiven you, and you won't die for this sin." **(David repents.)**

"But you have given great opportunity to the enemies of the Lord to despise and blaspheme him, so your child shall die."**(Consequence is painful.)**

David is unaware that this story is his story until Nathan pulls the mirror out when he says, This is you, David." It is at this point that David sees his reflection. This is known as a "mirrored reflection."

How does knowing about the "mirrored reflection" work in counseling folks today? Let's look and see how marriage is God's idea.

- <u>Rev 3:20</u>Behold. I stand at the door, and knock: if any (person) hear my voice, and open the door = **"mirrored reflection today is called <u>Engagement</u>."**

- <u>John 3:29</u>. The bride will go where the bride groom is = **"mirrored reflection" today is called the <u>Wedding.</u>**

- <u>Rev. 19:9</u> Marriage supper of the Lamb = **"mirrored reflection" today is called <u>wedding banquet.</u>**

- <u>Rev3:20b</u> I will come into him, and will sup with him, and he with me = **"mirrored reflection" today is called <u>marriage.</u>**

When a marriage goes sour for whatever reason, I have found that it is usually a reflection of their relationship with the Groom, Jesus Christ. Each individual must have a personal relationship with the Lord. Job's relationship with his wife was not good. "His wife said to him, "Are you still trying to be godly when God has done all this to you? Curse him and die." But he replied, "You talk like some heathen woman." Job 2:9-10

If just one spouse will connect with the Lord in a personal way (and this can take some time to prove to the Lord that this is a serious connection,) then God puts back the hedge of protection. This is proven in the story of Job, where Job said, "I used to know about you, but know, I know you and I repent in sack cloth and ashes." Peace, prosperity, health and well being for his family are Job's as we read that his marriage is up and running with seven sons and three daughters, he is healed, and he is prosperous. When we make contact with the Lord in a personal way, He is well pleased and will see to it that blessings start to fall once again.

Bill and Honey were in and out of their marriage four times and they were going to make one last effort for the sake of their six children. She indicated that he was a lazy bum hitting the couch as soon as he came home. According to Bill, she was a bossy, bickering hag. Another counselor and I concurred, it might be best to counsel them individually. The couple agreed this was a good idea.

Honey did have a story to tell. Taking care of seven young children, her husband included in the count, was more than she envisioned. She was exhausted with dark rings under her eyes. Her story unraveled like this: he was working and going to school to be a drug counselor, there was not enough money to cover buying clothes for the children or herself. Neither one had family in the area. They all attended church for three hours because the children were taken care of in Sunday school classes. She came to the Tuesday morning Bible study where having a baby sitter gave her some sense of freedom. Bill and Honey were religious people but had no idea of how to bring Jesus into their marriage. I could certainly sympathize with her story.

The husband's counseling ended with one session. The male counselor's advice was one of "maybe divorce was the answer." Certainly welfare could support the wife and children better than Bill and he could be free to get his schooling accomplished in peace and quiet. They separated but the wife wanted to continue counseling.

She confessed that life was much simpler without her husband, but the kids kept asking for their daddy. During the second session it was revealed that Honey was adopted as a baby and had an interest in finding her mother and family roots. On Sunday and Tuesday, she would drop the kids off at church then scoot out to research her past on the computer.

At the end of the third session I clued her in on having a personal relationship with the Lord and how to set up an appointment with him. Get alone, pull up a chair for you and the Lord, close your eyes and ask Him to sit with you, talk very little, then listen for His response. "Lord, I need your help," would be an example.

We made an appointment for the fourth meeting, but I told her we would not meet until she met the Lord. Time for the fourth session came. As I walked down the hall to meet her, I could see there was no change. "What happened?" "Nothing, I felt too weird," was her reply. "We have no appointment," I said, "Give me a call when it happens."

Two days later I got a call and I could tell from her voice that she met the Lord. She was at an "Aglow" meeting, sitting in the back, when she sensed His presence. She couldn't see him, but could hear His words. "You will be a family again. All will go well with you and your family. You must trust Me."

Things started to happen. Three days later her husband came home. No longer did he crash on the couch. He got involved in helping with the kids, sharing the responsibilities. New clothes for the kids and cans of food were left at their door.

Honey located her mother's relatives who knew where her mother lived. They were reunited as money came in for airfare. Not only that, but for three months out of the year she had a "work at home" job locating host homes for foreign students. This job went on for several years even after her husband graduated and was employed full time in his profession. They moved into their own home and started attending a smaller church where they both became involved in teaching classes.

This is the kind of fellowship that the Lord wants with

us and when that happens it's like Holy Glory envelops the individual and they become like a magnet. Honey actually freed her husband by depending and leaning on Jesus. She learned how to cast all of her cares upon Jesus rather than her husband.

This process of meeting Jesus works just the same if it is the husband that comes without the wife.

When folks leave Jesus out of center stage in their marriage, Satan just marches right in doing his job to destroy the family.

Chapter 9

Who Is Head of the Home?

Christians have been taught from the pulpit that wives are to submit to their husbands.

In counseling with couples, I am finding that the younger wives bristle at the thought of this concept.

Larry King, of the <u>Larry King Live</u>, program had an interesting discussion with prominent pastors on this topic. The program's purpose was to discuss the controversial bylaw changes of the Southern Baptists, concerning the addition of the phrase "wives will graciously submit to their husbands."

The participants were Rev. Mohler (Baptist Theological Seminary), Rev. Jerry Falwell (Liberty University –Southern Baptist), Rev. Robert Schuller (Crystal Cathedral) and Pat Ireland National Organization for Women representative.(NOW)

The scripture being referred to, but never read, was Ephesians 5:22 "Wives, submit yourselves unto your own husbands as unto the Lord." (NIV)

Rev. Schuller just couldn't relate to that scripture and pointed out that he personally would never use the scripture in his sermons. He was more for 2 Cor. 3:6b: "not of the letter, but of the spirit: for the letter killeth, but the spirit giveth life." (KJV) Indicating that the word "submit" is not a "happy" word. He recommends that a 60/40 relationship works best. Man as boss leads to headlock, 50/50 leads to deadlock, 60/40 leads to interlock. The interlock philosophy was unclear about who gets 60% and who gets 40%.

Rev. Jerry Falwell made his case that the headship of the husband was one of spiritual headship taking his family to church and making sure they were trained and taught the scriptures. He pointed out that his wife was smarter than he was and whenever they had a disagreement they did not proceed.

Pat Ireland of NOW was an interesting choice for the discussion of Biblical matters since she was not a Reverend, but she held her own in the discussion. Raising the point that the same book of Ephesians pointed out that slaves should submit to their masters. "Do you agree with that, Rev. Mohler?"

Rev. Mohler was adamant about the Southern Baptist's position in that the Bible is the inerrant word of God and wives are to submit graciously to their husband's leadership. And slaves (male or female) would be modeling what a good Christian is, when they submit to their masters, thus gaining the upper ground.

Somewhere along the line these learned folks missed the <u>topic sentence</u> which comes just before Ephesians 5:22 and that is 5:21 which states **"Submit to one another in fear of the Lord."**(KJV) or "out of reverence for Christ" (NIV). "One another" indicates that it is talking about more than one person, and sure enough it is talking about wife and husband. In order to tie in the topic sentence with the next sentence the word "submit" is used, "Wives submit to your husbands." When the next person is talked about the word for submit is love. <u>Eph. 5:25</u> "Husbands love your wives." The concluding sentence to the theme of husbands and wives is found in Eph. 5:33 "However, each one of you also must love his wife as he loves himself, and the wife must respect her husband."

If husbands and wives can submit to one another in fear of the Lord, there is a whole different understanding·of what submit, love and respect connotes. For "wives to submit graciously to the servant leadership of their husbands" doesn't have to be made into a bylaw, when husbands and wives are to love or submit to each other already.

I counseled with a husband who was so frustrated with his wife and the disrespect he was getting from his children that he was ready to leave. He was trying to get his wife to submit to him and she was rebelling against his authority and headship of the home. We talked about Eph. 5:21 and what he thought it implied. He had never understood it as the topic of Eph. 5:21-33.

I asked him who was head over him. He responded, "Jesus is." I asked, "If I were to ask your wife who was head over her, how would she reply?" "She loves Jesus." I talked about working together as partners, team players and let Jesus be head of the family. Very gently, I suggested that the disrespect the children were exhibiting toward him was possibly a mirrored reflection (God was allowing him to see and feel the pain) of his disrespect he was showing toward his wife. He was responsive to the possibility and agreed to change his attitude and behavior.

When he returned for the next counseling session, everything had changed. His comments were of victory. "It works, tension is gone, I don't have to be boss, we respect each other, the kids are fun to be with, it's like a dark cloud left our home, I enjoy coming home."

It is amazing how the atmosphere can change in a home when Jesus comes in as head of the family.

Can a curse be put on the son when the father leaves the family and the expression, "You are the man of the house now. Take care of your mother," is spoken?

An Asian mother with her fourteen-year-old son started attending our church. When I made a surprise visit to their apartment a loud argument was going on inside. The door opened, the son ran out and the mother invited me in. My first counseling session took place as she started to unravel her predicament with her son. Lee was truant from school and if he didn't return he would end up at a "Boy's Home."

Mae Ling was from Asia, leaving all relatives behind. The father / husband, who worked in the Middle East, came back to the States for only thirty days out of the year. His family lived in Montana. She spoke very little English. An Assembly of God church, in her hometown in Asia, lead her to the Lord.

For three years Mae Ling attended our church rather than an Asian Church because she wanted to force herself to understand English. During those years, her son was a delinquent around the apartments and schools. She would transfer him from one school to the next, to keep him at home. When the father came home - the son came home - no problems. When the father left chaos broke loose.

An emergency call came for me to come to her home. The son wanted to talk to me.

The mother left the home while we talked. It seems, the pressure of his mother needing him was too much and he couldn't stand it. She was smothering him. He didn't want to be the man of the house. He was torn between taking off and leaving her and his responsibility for his mom. When the mother came home, I could see the dependence and control she had over Lee.

An opportunity came for him to live with his Dad's family on their farm in Montana.

But Mae Ling wouldn't let him go without her. They left. The last report I heard was that mother and son had returned with the same scenario going on. The mother had purchased a new truck but would not let her 20-year-old son drive it. He took the keys, she laid down in front of the truck and he ran over her. Apparently she was not seriously injured.

It is my opinion that the head of the house needs to be Jesus Christ. To put a son in the position of head is destructive and sick. In this situation, I concentrated on the mother's pain and learned too late the root problem going on with the son.

As a Christian counselor, being able to reveal 'Spiritual Laws' that are broken is like delivering revelation knowledge to the counselee. Once they can see and are willing to proceed to correcting their relationship with the Lord, a confident client has hope their situation will be restored.

Basically it all centers around our relationship with Jesus. Once we get that corrected, our relationship with people (or what ever the problem) is cleared up. It is like the little demonic forces, who have come to steal, kill and destroy, have to leave because the Lord of Glory walks in. The "Shield of Protection" is restored over our country, our business, our family, and/or an individual.

Chapter 10

The Walking Wounded

Christians are expected to put on God's armor that will protect them from all strategies and tricks of Satan. Too many believers are oblivious to what their responsibilities are toward safeguarding themselves and their family. This is our armor: tell the truth, live righteously, share the gospel, have faith in God, be saved, read the Word of God and pray in the Spirit. (Eph:6:11-17) When the shield of faith comes down the fiery darts of Satan can come in and do a lot of damage. Damage can be every kind of sickness, disease and penetration known to man; bullets, accidents, bad family relationships, divorce, robbery, rape, kidnaping, cancer, HIV/AIDS and so on and so forth. And believers are oblivious to what went wrong.

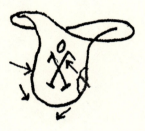

Illustration: # 3 Fiery dart gets in

For the "born again" believer, there is a corrective voice that will speak up to warn us "not that way, this way." Isa 30:21 "And if you leave God's paths and go astray, you will hear a Voice behind you say, 'No, this is the way; walk here.'"(TLB)

Humanistic Psychology is opposed to the idea of a sin nature and the Christian world has been influenced in this philosophy to the point today of ignoring the voice of correction. Hunt and McMahon rejected sin altogether and believed in the innocent child concept. Sigmund Freud and Carl Rogers denied the sinfulness of man; man is not responsible for what he does - someone else is responsible, man doesn't need divine revelation - he is sovereign and self-sufficient. The conclusion of Humanistic Psychology rationalizes that a person would not need to be "born again" if he was not a sinner who needed a Savior.

The word of God says that we have all sinned (found

guilty) and fallen short of the Glory of God. Hallelujah, we have a Savior who died to restore all who will respond and receive his forgiveness.. When we come into God's Kingdom we have a shield of protection that protects us, but it can be broken if we decide to ignore the voice of God and rebel. This doesn't mean we lose our salvation. It means we can be attacked by Satan.

Chapter 11

Consequences

To become knowledgeable about the Spiritual Laws that are placed in the Bible for our protection, we can avoid serious consequences. If we are not aware of them we can get hurt. The following are stories that reveal the consequences of breaking spiritual laws.

Consequence #1 <u>Critical Spirit</u>

In Numbers 13, Moses is instructed by God to send twelve spies into the promised land and search it out. Caleb and Joshua come back with a "Let us go up at once and possess the land for we are well able." The majority reported back that there were giants in the land and they felt like grasshoppers. As a result of this critical report, the people started to come against Moses. What happened to the ten spies who were faithless? <u>Num. 14:36</u> "Then the ten spies who had incited the rebellion against Jehovah by striking fear into the hearts of the people were struck dead before the Lord. Of all the spies, only Joshua and Caleb remained alive to go into the promised land."(TLB)

This little spiritual law is still in effect today. Eighth graders were notorious for moaning and groaning when an assignment in English was given out. One boy in particular was able to move the other students into complaining. I decided to read the story found in Numbers 13 to the whole class. What a difference it made; they stopped complaining.

Consequence # 2 <u>Anger/Resentment</u>

"So I want men everywhere to pray with holy hands lifted up to God, free from sin and anger and resentment." (1 Tim. 2:8)

This 2,000-year-old spiritual law has a modern day whammy. When my boys were about ten and twelve, the oldest son would tease the youngest. Usually he would just ignore the incident, but this particular evening, he hauled off and hit his brother in the mouth causing a regular blow up. I sent them off to their rooms to cool off. The next morning the youngest left for school. A few minutes later he came back with a bloody nose and a cut lip. He had fallen down the neighbor's steps. I was debating whether I should take him to the doctor, when he came up with solution. "Mom, let's pray." His prayer went something like this: "Father. I know exactly why this happened and I ask you to forgive me for getting mad at my brother last night and I am going to ask him to forgive me when he gets home from school. Thank you Father for healing me."

I removed the wash cloth from his lip and the once gruesome looking gash had stopped bleeding and the swelling had receded completely. A little bandage was all that was needed. When the boys got together after school, he asked his brother to forgive him. The boys started to pick up on these broken spiritual laws very quickly. It is interesting to note that the action caused the same reaction.

Consequence # 3 <u>Coveting Neighbor's Clothing</u>

Here is the spiritual law found in <u>Exod. 20:17</u> "You must not be envious of your neighbor's house, or want to sleep with his wife, or want to own his slaves, oxen, donkeys, or anything else he has."(TLB)

My oldest son had a job working for a big pipe supply warehouse. I got a call from the hospital one day telling me that he was in having X-rays of his foot. It seems a load of pipes had fallen and his foot got caught underneath. His dad and I rushed to the hospital praying in the spirit all the way. Thirty minutes later he came walking out looking a little white but ok.

I noticed a red, down-filled jacket draped over his arm. I

knew it didn't belong to our family. I had seen it at our home the day before and thought it belonged to one of his friends. After we hugged I asked him, "Who does the jacket belong to?" It seemed the jacket was left in our camper by the repairman. My son had wanted a down-filled jacket so he thought he would claim it for himself. This was the first day he had worn it and knew he had broken a spiritual law. He was anxious to get things corrected with the Lord and get the jacket back to its rightful owner. Can God be blamed for this accident or was my son's shield broken permitting the fiery dart of Satan to get in?

Consequence # 4 <u>Occult/Witches</u>

An usher tapped me on the shoulder just shortly before the end of the church service. I was called to help out with a woman in the back of the church. As I approached, I could see she was being tormented, pulling at her arms, trying to get something off her wrist and perspiring profusely. As we prayed, she threw back her head and grabbed for her throat. Whenever she tried to talk about the Holy Spirit, a lump came in her throat choking her. The question came up about her involvement with the occult. Reluctantly, she confessed that she wrote the horoscopes for her boyfriend's paper, but added, that she didn't believe in them. We read the Bible scriptures that forbid this kind of activity but she refused to believe that it was wrong.

A great deal of calamity came into her life as she related to me several years later at an evangelist tent meeting. It seems the Lord revealed to her the error of her ways. The scripture we used for her healing came from, <u>Duet. 18:10-13</u> "No Israelite (Christian) may practice black magic, or call on the evil spirits for aid, or be a fortune teller, or be a serpent charmer, medium, or wizard, or call forth the spirits of the dead." The Bible is up-to-date. This woman was tormented by an evil spirit until she renounced her activity and asked God to forgive her.

Consequence # 5 <u>Touching the Anointed of God</u>

Theological lectures became a bore to me and I discovered I wasn't alone. My pastor was discouraged at seeing the congregation dwindle away so he put out a questionnaire. I took it upon myself to really let him know where he was making his mistakes. With my superior attitude, I marked that questionnaire in haste. After all, I had a BA degree with Speech as my major and was an authority on these matters.

That evening I tossed and turned all night because of a pain in my big toe. My prayer was of the authoritarian type, "Pain, you have no right in my body, this is the temple of the Holy Spirit, I bind you Satan in the name of Jesus, you must leave." That conversation had no influence on my getting rid of the pain.

I wore a slipper to school until I could get an appointment with the doctor. His diagnosis was "Gout." I followed his prescription, but there was no relief. Saturday morning I was ironing clothes while listening to a Christian radio station. The preacher was talking about the story of Saul chasing David desiring to kill him. Saul went up into a cave to rest, while David, who was hiding in the very cave, snuck up on Saul and clipped off a portion of his robe. When Saul was down in the valley, David stepped out of the cave and waving the robe, shouted, "I could have killed you Saul, but I will not touch the anointed of God."

Hearing that message brought tears to my eyes. I knew what I had done. My pastor was anointed of God and I had no business sticking my nose (I mean my toe) into God's chosen one. When I asked God to forgive me, the pain left my toe instantly. That little lesson has saved me lots of pain.

Not only should we refuse to criticize Pastors and leaders but other Christians as well. Ps 105:15 "Touch not mine anointed, and do my prophets no harm." We really do get into hot water when we make critical remarks about God's anointed. It is as if we become God and decide what is best for that other person over there rather than taking care of our own business with the Lord. The Bible has quite a bit to say about this subject.

Matt 7:1-3 "Don't criticize, and then you won't be criticized. For others will treat you as you treat them. And why worry about a speck in the eye of a brother when you have a board in your own?" (TLB) I call this mirrored reflection.

A 9th grade student of mine wanted to borrow Katherine Kuhlman's book on <u>I Believe in Miracles.</u> One day, as I was getting ready to leave school, from behind the office counter I heard, "Thanks for letting me read Katherine Kuhlman's book. Wait and I will get it for you."

As I waited for the student, the secretary made her not-to-complimentary opinion be known about Miss Kuhlman in front of the student. The minute she made her remark I knew there was trouble ahead, and sure enough, the next day it was reported that the secretary had damaged her eye while picking up kindling for her fireplace. Interesting twist to this story was that it took her four weeks to recover and every morning she watched 700 Club during a time when Katherine Kuhlman was on the program. She was so moved by the program. She phoned the prayer line for healing.

A story that is not too familiar to Christian folks, found in 2 Kings 2:24, should give us an idea of how much power there is behind the person following after the Lord. Elijah was on his way to Jericho when some young boys started making fun of his bald head. As the story goes two female bears came out of the woods and ate up forty-two of the young fellows. I can just see the headlines today, "Forty-Two Boys Were Eaten Up By Bears."

Do you think the parents knew why their sons died? I don't think so, but, I do believe the story is there for parents to teach their children to watch what they say with their mouths. A person would learn to keep his mouth shut very quickly, if things like this were going on. The point is, I believe they are.

This next story was written up in the book "Women Get Out of the Box! You Are Called to the Ministry," by Katherine Schmidtke.

The first one I called about this project listened quietly and patiently while I told of the 'burning bush' experience I had with the Lord when I was in England in 1988 at a Rienhart Bonnke convention showing me in a vision the plat of land in Tacoma that I was to build a church, high school, and center on. The whole story took about eight minutes.

This was a man who was a mover and a shaker in the Christian community and a State worker. He and my husband grew up in the same church: we were in the same adult Sunday school class together, surely he would be a great help to propel this project forward.

His response pierced my heart. **"Do you know what they did in the Old Testament to faults prophets?"** "No, what do you mean?" **"They stoned them!"** The moment he made that comment to me, the thought ran through my head, "The stones will fall on you. You have ensnared yourself with these words. Can't you tell this project is of the Lord?"

Surely he was joking. Surely he could see the finger print of God on the vision and dream. Why would he take this attitude? I had forgotten that he didn't believe God could possibly use a woman in the ministry. Women were to stay home for the beckoned call of their husband and kids and be ornaments on their arms.

I remembered his comment so clearly one year later when the newspaper, radio and TV ran the story; 'Senator is Being Accused of Sexual Harassment by his Secretary.' He left the Senate a disgraced man.

Consequence # 6 <u>Disobedience</u>

A Disneyland trip found our family waiting in an hour long line to take a trip through the Pirates Cove. As we got closer to the entrance, a teenage girl crowded in front of us. My husband told her he didn't think it was right that all these people had waited over an hour and she just pushed her way in. She said something like, "Mind you own business."

She had just made that comment when she stuck her head through a window opening to shout to her friends who were getting on the boat. Pulling back, she ripped the top of her head opened as she scraped it past the pointed corner of a heavy iron lantern. Needless to say, she was taken out of line for repairs.

And we think spiritual laws aren't in operation today. Spiritual laws were meant to work for us, not against us. When people start to read the Bible and believe it to be the word coming from the Father, then lives are changed, their actions altered, healing comes and people are set free.

<u>NOTE</u>: Just let me interject this thought. Not all sick-nesses are as a result of sin (or broken spiritual laws). For we have the story in John 9:2 – "Master," His disciples asked Him, "why was this man born blind? Was it as a result of his own sins or those of his parents?" "Neither," Jesus answered. "But to demonstrate the power of God."

Another example is of Paul and his thorn in the flesh. Paul's thorn in the flesh wasn't healed. "Three different times I begged God to make me well again. Each time he said, "No. But I am with you; that is all you need. My power shows up best in weak people." The interesting thing about Paul was that he prayed three times for healing until he was satisfied with God's answer. Paul's thorn was to keep him deflated so he wouldn't get all puffed up over his third Heaven experience as cataloged in 2 Cor. 12:2-9. (TLB)

Consequence # 7 <u>Prayers: Good and Bad</u>

I had an experience with an accident in my brand-new car because of the way I prayed. Prayer was, "Lord, use this car for your Glory." Shortly after I was involved in an accident. A sixteen-year-old drove through a stop street, as a result I ran into the side of his car, banging up my fender, hood, and bumper. No one was hurt.

It is my belief that nothing can come my way that God doesn't allow. My first thought was, "Lord, reveal to me what I did to break my shield of protection." Nothing came to my understanding until four days later when I went to pick up my car. The assistant manager followed me out to the car. I could tell he had something on his mind.

"I want to tell you that I appreciated your bringing the car into our shop. Your bumper sticker spoke to my heart the very day I was ready to give up on life."

So that's what this accident was all about. My "Hurting? God Cares" sticker was needed by the Lord to help a Christian brother whose life was hitting the skids. When I think back, it was just a few days before the accident that I dedicated the car to the Lord to use for His Glory in any way He thought fitting. This accident cost me not a cent, the half day I spent getting an estimate I talked to a lady about Jesus Christ and the car was as good as new. Rom. 8:28 "And we know that all that happens to us is working for our good if we love God and are fitting into his plans." (TLB)

From this experience I learned to pray differently. "Lord, thank you for this car. Keep me and all those around me safe whether driven or parked. Amen"

Margie had a prodigal daughter, who ran away from home, got married to an older, abusive man, and became pregnant. For several years Margie's prayer was, "Oh, God, Do anything you have to do to bring my daughter home." Though her prayer was answered Margie confessed on a Christian TV program that her prayer could have been stated in a different way.

Her daughter came home paralyzed from an automobile accident where she was thrown out of the car cracking her head on the curb. Neither the baby nor the husband were harmed. The husband abandoned his wife and their child. The prodigal came home with a repentant heart. Twenty years later, the daughter walked with some restrictions and the baby is married with children, all "born again" Christians.

Here is another example of prayer answered but with tragic results. The parents prayed this prayer for their prodigal son. "Take him to the edge of Hell if you have to Lord, but bring him to Jesus."

The newspaper wrote up the story of a twenty two-year old male driver burned in the cab of his truck, teetering over the edge of the bridge.

This is my personal opinion. I think we need to watch what we say with our mouth.

"Lord Jesus, reveal yourself to my daughter or son and bring her/him home safe and sound." Simple and to the point.

This is a story coming out of a Campus Crusade letter concerning witnessing to the Muslims in the Middle East. "When we witness to someone, we pray and ask God to give them a vision of Jesus . . . and He does! Eighty percent of everyone converting from Islam to Christianity in the Middle East has had a vision of Jesus.

The three Muslim men told a worker of having experienced a powerful vision. They saw a man with a radiant face. He was clothed in a robe of pure white and surrounded by a brilliant light of glory. He told them. "I am Jesus. I am the true way. You need to believe the Bible and believe in Me."

They found a Bible, studied it, discovered God's way of salvation and gave their lives to Christ. Seventeen Muslims are now studying the Bible with them.

The way we pray makes a difference.

Consequence # 8 <u>A Broken Spirit</u>

<u>Prov 17:22</u> A merry heart doeth good like a medicine: but a broken spirit (heart) drieth the bones (or makes one sick). (KJV)

My best friend's husband and youngest son died in a private airplane accident. This was devastating news to her as it would be to most folks. Even though she put up a good front, life lost a lot of its zest for her. She filled her life with the remaining three children and was involved with the work that she and her husband had built up. She decided to go to college and got involved in the ministry. On one of her visits home, and in confidence, she wanted me to pray for her as she had a blood disease that was life threatening. With the doctor's predictions she knew what she had done. Immediately she tried to put into effect the "merry heart" concept, but the enemy had gained a foot hold and a wonderful Christian friend went home to be with the Lord at a young age.

Dr. Norman Cousins has written a book called "Anatomy of An Illness" which is his story of killing cancer with laughter, vitamins and accentuating the scripture, that says, a "merry heart doeth good like medicine."

Evelyn was another one who had her spirit broken. As

a widow with limited funds, going to Hawaii was out of the question, so when her sister presented the idea that they would like her to join them, she was overjoyed. For some reason their relationship was strained and they left without her.

The last time I saw Evelyn, her hair was falling out from the radiation treatments that she was taking for cancer. The doctor gave her a no hope verdict, but I came to pray for her healing. I brought along some Flip Wilson and Bill Cosby records to cheer her up.

The Lord gave me a word of knowledge concerning her illness. I called Evelyn the next day to let her know about the word I was given. The experience had to do with a tea cup that turned into a wooden Hawaiian mug which fell apart at the bottom, spilling out maggots. I asked if the word Hawaii meant anything to her. She could not think of anything.

Three days after her funeral I got a call from Evelyn's sister. Apparently the word Hawaii had a great deal to do with their coldness toward each other. Their relationship was cleared up and healed once they knew that God revealed the problem to a so-called stranger. The fiery dart came in quickly and did its damage.

In my way of thinking, this could have been avoided by believing that all things work together for good to those who are called according to God's purpose.

Consequence # 9 <u>Getting Involved With Things of This World</u>

I was experiencing a rash of prank calls from a group of high school girls. The four letter words that spewed out of their mouths were atrocious. I believe God will not allow anything or anyone to come my way without His permission.

Job 1:10 says that the believer has a hedge around them and Satan can't attack us unless the hedge is taken down. 1John 5:18 backs that up with "For Christ holds him securely and the devil can't get his hands on him." So my thinking was that the Lord wanted me to witness to these girls. Every time they called I shared the Kingdom of God with them. Still, they called. Joining together with other Christians we bound Satan. Still, calls came.

Saturday morning, after a call came in, I sat down and asked the Lord what the problem was. "Broken shield," came the reply. "How have I broken my protective shield?" Instantaneously I knew what it was. I started to review the words the girls were using and discovered they were the very words that were used in the video tape of "Saturday Night Fever." It hadn't dawned on me when I picked it up that it was "R" rated. But as I watched the movie it was definitely "R" rated.

I knew what I had to do. And, as soon as I got it out of my house and asked the Lord to forgive me for even bringing it into my home the calls stopped. Can you understand that? The calls stopped. Satan gets a free hand when a spiritual law is broken but he could only grow what I had planted.

Consequence # 10 <u>Perverted Sex</u>

Do you think God doesn't care what we are putting into our minds? I think He does. My son called me down to his room on Saturday morning with this question, "Mom, did you take the two hundred dollars that I left on the top of the dresser?" We looked all over for his money which he had saved in preparation to buy his own truck.

"Where exactly did you leave it on the dresser?" He pointed out the back left edge. As I looked down on the floor and just underneath the dresser, I noticed a catalogue that displayed women's clothing and lingerie. My son was beet red.

I must say that the catalogue companies are getting a bit pornographic in their advertising. At any rate I asked him, "Why did you feel you had to hide this book?" Actually, I really didn't have to say anything because he knew what law he had broken and that the money was gone forever. He asked me to pray with him about his attitude he was falling into. Interestingly enough that very day he and his dad went to buy a small truck which ended up costing him $200.00 less than he had anticipated having to pay for it.

Do you think this type of girly exposure is normal, healthy growth for a sixteen-year-old? Well, the Bible indi-cates we should flee from such things (Prov. 4:23)

I personally find this story to be amazing. As a mother and father we didn't have the slightest idea what was going on with the girly magazine. The circumstance that stopped this activity had to have been orchestrated by the Lord. And when the magazine was exposed and repented of, God forgave my son and gave him a blessing. I think that is totally amazing.

A wonderful Christian friend of mine worked for a Christian boss, who made it a practice of sneaking up behind the women who worked for him and pressed his body parts against them. Guess what he came down with? He died of Prostrate cancer. This was a classic case of the fiery dart of Satan getting in the door that was opened.

Consequence # 11 <u>Someone Has Aught Against You</u>

I had an interesting experience with another worker at church. We were involved in the cleanup of our new church building. At the end of each cleaning session there would be refreshments supplied by a gracious host.

One night I stopped by for some punch. Small talk took over and I thought I would give the hostess a compliment that went something like this: "Some people have a real talent for hosting – that doesn't seem to be mine." That comment hit her like a ton of bricks. I got busy talking to some other folks and then left. The next cleaning day she avoided me all together and wouldn't say a thing.

I started to develop a plugged up nose which became irritated every time I was exposed to dust so I had to curtail my cleaning days. However, I did see her again when we dropped our children off at church. Being a friendly person, I tried to start a conversation with her. Without results. I thought to myself, 'if you want to be that way, okay. That's your problem.'

My plugged up nose wasn't getting better. I cast the sickness out, bound Satan, I joined together with others in prayer, anointed with oil. Nothing happened. For three weeks this thing hung on.

One Sunday, the head of the work crew asked me why he hadn't seen me. I told him about my nose problem. His advice for me was to take vitamin A and Zinc and in three days it would be gone. "Now we were on the right track," I thought.

A whole week went by – nothing. As a child of God I knew that I could get healing so I asked the Lord what was holding up the healing. What was I doing wrong? He told me. And it was the very thing He had told me in the beginning – four weeks earlier. "You must go to the church woman and ask her forgiveness." I kept putting it out of my mind because surely it was her problem, not mine.

Matthew 5:23 says, "So if you are standing before the altar in the Temple, offering a sacrifice to God, and suddenly remember that a friend has aught against you, leave your sacrifice there beside the altar and go and apologize and be reconciled to him."(TLB)

I knew what I had to do but I wasn't anxious to do it. I finally agreed that healing was better than all these nasal sprays and headaches. Once I started to dial her number, I knew I would be healed.

Our conversation brought tears to both of our eyes and reconciliation came. Three days later "A" and Zinc kicked in and I was completely healed from my nose problem.

It's interesting that I could have been healed in the very beginning but my stubbornness took me all around the mountain instead of over it. It was a good lesson for me. I never want to go through that again. It's just not worth it.

Consequence # 12 <u>Death Wish</u>

<u>Prov 6:2b</u> "ensnared by the words of your mouth," (NIV)

I counseled with a woman who was diagnosed with lymphoma cancer. As we talked, I was impressed to ask if she had expressed with her mouth a death wish. Big tears weld up in her eyes as she told me eight days before she had been diagnosed with cancer, she wanted to die. It seems that she was in a situation of caring for the elderly so her husband could stay in the ministry and she hated the job. The Bible indicates that we are ensnared by the words of our mouth. The enemy got through a hole she had opened in her shield, but now, she did not want to die, she wanted to live.

Our prayer was one of asking the Lord to forgive her for her death wish and cleanse her once again with His blood.

The next step was to curse the root of the cancer and command it to go. Often doctors are used at this point to bring about the healing medicine, as was true in this case. Life and death are in the power of the tongue and so often we confess the negative rather than the positive.

Consequence # 13 <u>Sowing Seeds of Destruction</u>

<u>Job 4:7b</u> "Experience teaches that it is those who sow sin and trouble who harvest the same."(TLB)

A trip to Hawaii was interrupted with a trip to the hospital and the word of three broken bones. Hawaii, with its great balmy weather, makes it conducive to walking in the evening breeze. My son had just crossed the street and I was following several strides behind when all of a sudden my foot caught in the cracked curb and threw me into the street as if I was diving into a pool except my hands were bound to my sides. On the way down, enough time transpired to know this was going to hurt. I smashed flat on my nose and mouth. An ambulance was called to take me to the hospital. "Thank you, Jesus, Thank you, Jesus." was my prayer. X-rays revealed I had a broken nose, fractured right elbow, and a fractured left foot. We left the hospital with pain pills, a sling, and a temporary cast for my foot and with the words to return in two days for more x-rays on the nose.

I took a couple of Advil and went to sleep. I slept through the night awaking early in the morning with this question on my heart. "Oh, Lord, how did I break my shield?" His answer was immediate and in one word that spoke volumes to me. "Table."

What did table mean? Before we left for Hawaii, we were moving our church from a large office space to a store front building. This was the responsibility of my youngest son while I was taking a much needed vacation with my oldest son and his family. In moving to the office space we stored much of our furniture and church paraphernalia so we were down to not much to move to the store front. The office space was owned by a cantankerous man who froze us out on Sunday and Wednesday nights and refused to let us touch nor would he change his computerized heating system.

A table was used that didn't belong to the church, but I thought it would certainly make a fine addition to our inventory. I decided the owner could determine whom it belongs to - them or us. He conceded that it must belong to us. The night of the accident was the day my son's crew moved the furniture to the store front. I knew what I had done and what I must do about it. I asked the Lord to forgive me and to wash me clean in his blood. Taking that table back was uppermost in my mind. That would have to wait until we got back home.

Healing came so fast I had my son take pictures of me with two black eyes, so I could give a message on the things we do to break our shield of protection. The before and after x-rays of my nose two days later showed my nose had been healed.

When I got home, the table went back to its proper owner. The interesting part of this story is that when we got our tables from storage, all five tables that were perfect when they went in, were damaged either with scratches or edge dents - only one remained unscathed.

I am not proud of this story, but I leaned a great lesson. Many times I could have escaped the route that I took but I was the one who opened the hole in my shield of protection and the Lord was there all the time saying, "No, not that way." The enemy's fiery dart came in and did a lot of damage. Sowing seeds of destruction can hurt.

Consequence # 14 <u>Idols</u>

<u>Acts 17:30</u> "God tolerated man's past ignorance about these things, but now he commands everyone to put away idols and worship only Him." <u>1 John 5:21</u> "Keep yourself from idols." <u>Jer. 4:1-2</u> "if you put away these idols - I will bless you." Ezek. 14:7

"Idols cut you off from God." (TLB)

I want to fortify this message with scripture on this particular subject because many people are rather protective of their collections. And there are folks who don't know what an idol might be or look like. A message given by Pastor Benny Hinn woke me up to the things we bring into our house and the jewelry we innocently wear that can give us problems.

Ezekiel 8:1-8 "Ezekiel is taken by the hair to the Temple and saw the wickedness. " <u>Ezek. 8:9-10</u> "Go in," he said, "and see the wickedness going on in there!" So I went in. The walls were covered with pictures of all kinds of snakes, lizards, and hideous creatures, besides all the various idols worshiped by the people of Israel. (TLB) In Chapter nine it goes on to describe how God cleanses the temple and land of the leaders and people who worshiped the images.

Is it possible that we are bringing idols into our homes that are actually causing death, disease and sickness to our family members? A good friend of mine told me about her dad who had a sudden swelling on one side of his chin and wanted me to pray for him. The moment I saw him, the word "frog" came to my mind. I simply prayed that the swelling would go as quickly as it had grown.

Cancer was the doctor's prognosis. He was operated on immediately and exploratory surgery brought complications of nine more operations. His esophagus was torn so he couldn't eat through the mouth. Different entries were tried to feed him liquids - only the stomach proved effective. I was given this report along with the fact that they set him aside to die.

These were fine Christian people and they needed help from the Lord. One morning I came up out of bed with a word of knowledge from the Lord. "Buddha." They must have a Buddha in the house along with frogs. I went to the hospital with that piece of news for the wife.

The wife, who is Japanese, married an American soldier.

Sure enough, they had lots of frogs (she had a whole collection of them) along with one Buddha (but didn't worship it). I was confident we hit the nail on the head and if they would get rid of the items her husband would recover. They were not convinced.

Several weeks went by with continual reports that he was not going to last. My son, who had a little influence on this family, convinced them to check out the idols. Several years before, I had done two TV programs dealing with the idols we have in our homes and their effects on our well being. They agreed to watch them.

I lugged the TV and tape recorder to the ninth floor and played the videos in his room.

The wife was totally convinced she needed to get rid of the frogs and Buddha. I happened to say that if they were willing to get rid of the idols that in three days they would see signs of improvement in her husband. Jer. 4:1-2 says if you put away these idols - I will bless you. A thirty gallon can of smashed frogs and one Buddha went to the garbage that very day.

When we met at the hospital the next day she brought out a, two inch flat, black stone with a white lamb on the front. She wanted to know if that was okay. I looked and on the back, in gold letters, something was written in Japanese, so I asked what it said. Kind of sheepishly, she said "Double luck." I told her I didn't think it was working. She reached in her purse and pulled out a duplicate and smashed them both on the floor.

Three days later the doctors saw such improvement in Don they decided to make plans for radiation. The man was healed of cancer but the toll was heavy. He lost a rib, all of his teeth were removed, his body is very leathery in the areas around the chest.

God was not finished with this family yet. The house was not quite clean. I got a call from his daughter - he was back in the hospital - blood clots were threatening his life and he would be operated on in three days - would I come and pray for him?

"This guy can't die now, Lord - what is going on?" Once again the Lord responded with "The heart of the home is clogged." I called the wife to ask her what she considered the heart of her home (living room, bedroom, kitchen?) Without hesitating she acknowledged that it was the kitchen. There was something in the kitchen that was plugging things up. I continued to ask her questions about her kitchen. She finally responded that she had seventeen plants in a very small space actually climbing up the walls. It was a jungle.

I told her if she would get rid of some of the plants or trim them back, I would come and pray for her husband before he was operated on and I was confident the Lord would heal him. I remember saying something like: heathens cut their bodies and your husband is not a heathen. So, let's do what we have to do to bring healing. I couldn't believe I said that. It wasn't received with open arms because she wasn't interested in getting rid of her plants at all.

I went to the hospital and asked the wife to show me

where the plants were located. I wanted to make sure this was the problem. She drew a diagram for me. The interesting thing was when she opened up the sheet of paper, on the other side was the doctor's drawing that he had made for the wife showing her where the blood clots were and it was the exact same configuration she made for me showing where her plants were located in her kitchen. Every place she had a plant was the very place there was a blood clot. It was rather amazing. This was so obvious to me that the Lord was speaking that I went in to pray for Don before the plants were gone.

I was sure she would rush home and trash all the plants. A few of the plants were placed outside but not with any enthusiasm and when the husband came home from the hospital, with all blood clots gone, he was not supportive of removing any plants from the house. I was mud in their eyes for a good six months.

He was not able to eat any thing solid. It was Ensure from a drip that kept him alive. Only after they removed the plant that was taking over was he able to eat solid food. So remarkable was his motivation to eat, after the plant was removed, the wife confessed to me that she had made an idol out of the plant and even had a pet name for it.

This message is not always well received and is best read or preached about rather than being specific to the person that may or may not have idols in their life. A person who wants to help can come across like Job's friends or can be treated as Jesus was treated when he made a specific effort to find the man he had healed by the Pool of Bethesda. Jesus told him not to sin anymore or perhaps a worse sickness would come upon him. Apparently he liked his sin just like people today like their idols; whatever they might be.

I wonder sometimes about my Scandinavian friends who bring into their homes the Trolls from the European countries that are just "cute creatures attached to the fables of their homeland." I walked into a home of a woman who had lost three husbands. At the age of forty-seven one dropped dead of a massive heart attack right in front of her while he was talking to her. One dropped dead as he was walking up the steps to the home. Another died eight years after her second marriage. Interesting thing about the mantel in her home, the three large trolls from Norway were center stage.

Another woman was shown what the scriptures say about bringing idols into her home. Isaiah 43:12 "whenever you have thrown away your idols, I have shown you my power." It was suggested that perhaps the trolls and pixies she had in her home and around her yard were causing the healing that she needed for her back to be held up. What Christian wants to be told that they have something in their home that might displease the Lord and cause damage to them and their families

If you check out a library book on the subject of Scandinavian trolls, they are listed under titles like witches and trolls. From the children's library you can read all about the trolls of Norway. One troll wants to steal the babies (one reason why the Lutherans of Norway want to baptize their babies right away), another one wants to be the head of the house (putting a troll on the mantel would not be a good idea), and one is a regular tease in the water. It is not that these idols (trolls, elves, etc.) have any power but the stories behind them are known by the enemy and if we bring them into our home, we open up a hole in our shield giving the enemy an opportunity to jump right in.

Webster's Dictionary has these definitions for witches, trolls, elves, pixies and etc.:

Elf = a mythological being, commonly a sprite, often frail and diminutive, including sprite, pxies, mermaids, mermen, nixes, dwarfs, incubi, and succubus.

- Sprite = a shade, ghost, apparition, and elf, fairy, goblin.
- Pixies = English folklore - a mischievous sprite or fairy.
- Mermaid / Merman = Fabled marine creature, woman's or man's body with a fish tail.
- Nixes = A water sprite - part man or woman - part fish.
- Dwarf = troll.
- Troll = A supernatural being, conceived sometimes as a dwarf, sometimes as a giant, fabled to inhabit caves, hills and like places.
- Incubi = an evil spirit, supposed to lie upon persons in their sleep and to have sexual intercourse with women by night, nightmare.

- Succubus = A demon, a female form to have sexual intercourse with men in their sleep. Notice: these are classified as Elves.

I remember looking through the viewer of the TV camera I was practicing with. I was focused on a statue of a boy in velvet pants leaning on a tree stump. When looking closer, I noticed he had pointed ears. He was an elf! As expensive as that thing was, I took the sledge hammer to it - destination: garbage can. Quite frankly, I believe God allowed me to see that accursed thing I had in my house, because I was just starting a TV production co. called "The Lion of Judah" ministry and I knew God would not be able to anoint the programs if I had this idol in my home.

I was called to the hospital by the mother of a twelve-year-old boy who was recovering from an emergency appendectomy. His healing was taking longer than normal and needed to be prayed for. For a husky boy he looked pail and limp. When I finished praying, I noticed a small ball with a hideous face of a troll on the surface. I asked him what he was doing with it. A friend had given it to him when he came to visit. I told him if he got rid of the ball, God would heal him immediately. He walked out of the hospital the next day miraculously healed, according to the mother.

Oh, that we would have a public bonfire as they did in Acts 19:18-19 and get rid of our idols as we are stirred by God's message.

Consequence # 15 <u>Belong to Pagan Organization</u>

A dentist responded to the Lord once it was known that he could die of the cancer that filled his body. The Lord revealed himself to Mark, in a marvelous way filling him with the Holy Spirit. The cancer disappeared for months. Then it returned.

You could see his neck was swollen so he could not button his collar and was progressing quickly. After dinner his wife took my hand and wanted to know if perhaps a curse his aunt had spoken against him could be causing the cancer. The minute she said the word curse, the Lord spoke a word into my mind.

I asked her if her husband was a member of a secret fraternal organization, for that was the word I received. Her response was yes. I recommended that they watch a video tape exposing the organization for what it really believes. They watched the tape. He removed the emblems from his car, renounced his membership, asked God to forgive him and got washed in the blood of Jesus. We then prayed for his healing. The last report I heard was that his cancer was receding.

The secret organization he belonged to was one of salvation through good works rather than through Jesus Christ. According to the video put out by Jeremiah films on "Free Masonry" 1991, it is a secret society that has similar rituals to that of witchcraft ceremonies. They are blindfolded, robed, a sword tip pierces their chest, must pledge they will keep secret of all that goes on, must swear to the Egyptian trinity, all done before the "worshipful master."

Lucifer is known as their god of light and other Pagan activities are ever present in their symbols. Jesus is just one among many gods. "Masons don't need a savior. They are saved by their society." They believe in the broad way to heaven when Jesus talks about the narrow way. <u>Matt 7:13</u> "Heaven can be entered only through the narrow gate! The highway to hell is broad, and its gate is wide enough for all the multitudes who choose its easy way. (TLB)

I ministered to a Junior High student who belonged to an Auxiliary group, who was tormented in her spirit when she wanted to leave the organization. A father, who belonged to the Masons, angrily confronted me when I shared the Gospel with his seventeen-year-old son.

<u>Matt 4:10</u> " Jesus told him. The Scriptures say, 'Worship only the Lord God. Obey only him.'" <u>Isa 57: 7b</u> "Behind closed doors you set your idols up and worship someone other than me. This is adultery, for you are giving these idols your love instead of loving me." (TLB)

Some "rock concerts" can be classified as Pagan gatherings. John Achord, out of curiosity, "to see what a rock concert was like," stepped into Satan's trap when he attended a group called "Rush" on June 18, 1984 at the Tacoma Dome. The story came out of the <u>News Tribune,</u> "Kidnaping and Assault at the Rush Rock Concert." The article reported what happened. "Police believe Achord, 22, was killed in a remote area of the city sometime May 19, after he disappeared from a rock concert, the first he had ever attended. He was stabbed to death with a double-edged hunting knife a murder victim whose headless body was found near Elbe."

His mother and brothers indicated that he had just recently been baptized at the Baptist Church he attended and would "preach" to anyone that would listen.

The Bible talks about a wedding feast prepared for his guests. Interesting point to this story is that of all the guests that were there, one was a standout and very obvious to the father of the groom, he didn't belong because he wasn't wearing the proper attire provided for him.

The Kingdom of Heaven is described in Matt 22:1, 11-13. "For instance," he said, "it can be illustrated by the story of a king who prepared a great wedding dinner for his son.

But when the king came in to meet the guests, he noticed a man who wasn't wearing the wedding robe [provided for him]. "'Friend,' he asked, 'how does it happen that you are here without a wedding robe?' And the man had no reply. "Then the king said to his aides, 'Bind him hand and foot and throw him out into the outer darkness where there is weeping and gnashing of teeth.'"(TLB)

Was that the case with John Achord, only he attended the enemy's party? John was washed in the blood of the Lamb. His outfit was white. A standout in comparison to the crowd's dingy gray, Is it possible that Satan looked over the rock concert attenders and discovered someone with a white garment and told his henchman to, "Get him!"

Did the counterfeiter take advantage of a new Christian

who was just "curious" about what went on in the enemies camp and die early?

Consequence # 16 <u>Not Tithing</u>

What a blessing tithing is. It is a spiritual law that God has set in place to prosper the person who understand its principles and follows through with joyfully participating.

Physical health, employment success, family harmony, and financial blessings are all tied up in this one law. The actual definition of the word tithe means ten percent (10%). Tithing is set in place to remind us to put God first, take care of His pastors, place of worship and to the spreading of the Gospel. <u>Deut. 14:23c</u>. The purpose of tithing is to teach us always to put God first in our lives. Choosing not to partici-pate classifies the person as a robber.

> <u>Mal 3:8-11</u> "Will a man rob God? Surely not! And yet you have robbed me. What do you mean? When did we ever rob you? You have robbed me of the tithes and offerings due to me. And so the awesome curse of God is cursing you, for your whole nation has been robbing me. Bring all the tithes into the storehouse so that there will be food enough in my Temple; if you do, I will open up the windows of heaven for you and pour out a

blessing so great you won't have room enough to take it in! Try it! Let me prove it to you! Your crops will be large, for I will guard them from insects and plagues. Your grapes won't shrivel away before they ripen," says the Lord Almighty." (TLB)

This is what happens when we rob God according to Prov 6:30 "Excuses might even be found for a thief if he steals when he is starving! But even so, he is <u>fined seven times</u> as much as he stole, though it may mean selling everything in his house to pay it back."

Imagine there are ten pennies laid out in a row. To tithe on those ten pennies you would remove one penny. That one penny you give to the Lord would be replaced by God opening the windows of heaven to bless you. But if you decided not to give the one penny, you will put into motion the lose of seven pennies and have only three for yourself. Some of the ways to lose would be that you or your kids get sick, the washing machine breaks down, someone steals from you, the possibilities are endless.

Anne maxed out her credit card and was five thousand dollars in debt with no visible way of getting free from the burden. One Saturday, as she was listening to Christian TV, the words, "test me and see if I will not pour out a blessing so great you will not be able to take it in." She sent in a check to Trinity Broadcasting Network (TBN) for $50.00. Monday morning, when she arrived at work, her boss called her in wanting to let her know he was raising her salary five thousand dollars a year.

The miracle continued for Anne. She and her son lived in a one bedroom apartment, but needed a two bedroom. A big rain storm caused her apartment to be flooded and the only other one available was a two bedroom on the second floor given to her at the same price as the one bedroom. God proved himself to Anne as he will to all who tithe with a right attitude.

My brother tells his story of testing God out in his tithing. He had been a church goer for a long time, but thought he could get away with a couple of dollars when the offering plate was passed. After all, it was his money, he worked for it.

His opportunity came when he was trying to sell his home. It was looking very desperate after three months went into six. The Sunday morning he decided to start tithing he came home to find a real-estate lady with a buyer ready to sign the papers. Not only has he been faithful to tithing, his walk with the Lord is a lifestyle change.

<u>Luke 6:38</u> "For if you give, you will get! Your gift will return to you in full and overflowing measure, pressed down, shaken together to make room for more, and running over. Whatever measure you use to give–large or small–will be used to measure what is given back to you." Why would a person possibly want to rob God of His tithes and offerings?

Consequence # 17 <u>Breaking a Vow or Promise</u>

It is interesting to see how easy it is to break a vow today especially in the wedding vow that spouses make to each other, before God and witnesses. Thinking "divorce" is the solution. The covering that God puts over a married couple is broken at the time of divorce and the enemy couldn't be happier. Take a look at the damage.

A book written by Glenn T. Stanton titled, <u>The Broken Promises of Divorce</u> reiterates that divorced individuals are three times more likely to commit suicide than married. Divorced women suffer twice as many injuries as married and women have an increased risk of assault. Divorced men are nine times more likely to die of tuberculosis and four times more likely to die of diabetes than married men."

Children of divorce are at a greater risk for poverty, health problems, alienation and antisocial behavior, sixty-two percent no longer identify with the faith of their parents, increase of dropping out of high school, need psychological help and 40 times more likely to experience child abuse. <u>Americans for Divorce Reform</u> indicated that divorce was still visible twelve to twenty-two years later in a child's life.

The male prison population has these characteristics, according to Hudson Institute study. Seventy percent of the adult population grow up without a father, 60 percent are rapists. Seventy-five percent of adolescents charged with murder grew up without a father.

Certainly God is showing us through all the statistics

that have been collected on the subject of divorce that to break the marriage vow or any vow brings hurt, pain and destruction to the family of God.

I had an opportunity to run across, in two different situations, extremely wealthy men who promised to give 1.5 million dollars apiece to a non-profit organization that was going to build a church, high school and center in an area that they were both familiar with. They had once owned large portions of acreage in the same area. The one man was older and was so interested that he and his wife were willing to go into their private funds to see the program started. The other man was a wealthy philanthropist whom I met years ago at the college we both had attended. He also promised 1.5 million dollars immediately.

Three million would be used to buy the acreage, clear the land and build the first phase. At the time of its beginning, the total cost would be 15 million dollars. The acreage was prime property besides being zoned for the purpose it was intended and needed to be purchased immediately. We started the church fully expecting the word of these men to be honored.

The day of collecting was put off by the older gentleman because a young man, who was a land developer, slipped in with a need for five million dollar to build a shopping mall in another city. Two years later he went bankrupt. A five million dollars loss meant we would have to wait. For seven years we were promised it would come but it never did.

Every time I went to meet with my wealthy college

friend, he talked about the losses he was going through with his radio stations. This in reality had nothing to do with the foundation's funds that the 1.5 million dollars would come from but his personal wealth was taking a hit.

Uncle Bud came to our rescue and promised to give one million dollars. He would have it in thirty days. The owners of the property we wanted to buy decided to split the acreage up so the property would cost eight hundred thousand dollars. We felt this could actually work.

After seven years of hearing their promises to produce the money, the property we wanted for the Lord was purchased by a large building conglomerate for homes.

We were disappointed in the lack of responsibility for making a promise and then not keeping it. We learned later that the spiritual consequences that are built in came upon each one.

Each one of the wealthy men lost much more than we were asking for and Uncle Bud who was coming in at the last minute to help us, but never did, lost his home to methamphetamine his son was cooking up in the basement.

Eccl. 5:4-6 "So when you talk to God and vow to him that you will do something, don't delay in doing it, for God has no pleasure in fools. Keep your promise to him. It is far better not to say you'll do something than to say you will and then not do it. In that case, your mouth is making you sin. Don't try to defend yourself by telling the messenger from God that it was all a mistake [to make the vow]. That would make God very angry; and he might destroy your prosperity."

Consequence # 18 <u>Forgetting to Tell Them</u>

Paul made two very interesting statements having to do the ministry God called him to, found in Acts 18:6 "But when the Jews opposed him and blasphemed, hurling abuse at Jesus, Paul shook off the dust from his robe and said, "Your blood be upon your own heads— I am innocent— from now on I will preach to the Gentiles." And in <u>Acts 20:26-28</u> "Let me say plainly that no man's blood can be laid at my door, **for I didn't shrink from declaring all God's message to you. "And now beware! Be sure that you feed and shepherd God's flock**— his church, purchased with his blood— **for the Holy Spirit is holding you responsible as overseers."**(TLB)

We, as Christians are responsible for telling others about the Good News of the Gospel and to disciple and train the new converts. What happens when we refuse to tell or teach others about Jesus?

Evelyn Kelly was in and out of the hospital for years with stomach problems. Migraine headaches controlled her life. One day she heard a message on walking out of your illness by doing what God wants you to do. She made up her mind that she would start to teach a Bible study class. Her prayer was simple, "Lord if you want me to teach this class you are going to have to heal me other wise their blood will be upon you, not me." She has been teaching for twenty-five years never having a migraine or stomach problem.

Paul was referring to <u>Ezekiel 3:18, 21</u>. If you refuse to warn the wicked when I want you to tell them, "You are under the penalty of death; therefore repent and save your life," they will die in their sins, but I will punish you. I will demand your blood for theirs. But if you warn him and he repents, he shall live, and you have saved your own life too."

Keeping the Hedge up

Heavy unexpected discipline comes when we open the door seemingly innocently. More often than not we blame God for allowing bad things to happen to us. Ignorance of spiritual laws is each individual's responsibility to learn about.

For example, see if you can find the spiritual law in the act of taking communion. Taking communion has a built in spiritual law that most people are not cognizant of - the (blessing) ability to be healed, or God's judgment.

1 Cor. 11:27-30 So if anyone eats this bread and drinks from this cup of the Lord in an unworthy manner, he is guilty of sin against the body and the blood of the Lord. That is why a man should examine himself carefully before eating the bread and drinking from the cup. For if he eats the bread and drinks from the cup unworthily, not thinking about the body of Christ and what it means,

he is eating and drinking God's judgment upon himself; for he is trifling with the death of Christ. That is why many of you are weak and sick, and some have even died. (TLB)

An unworthy manner has to do with what? It has to do with not taking communion until we know what Jesus' beating was for. **How does what he went though affect me today when I take communion?** This is what he did for you. Isa 52:14. They shall see my Servant beaten and blood-ied, so disfigured one would scarcely know it was a person standing there. So shall he cleanse many nations. (Or, many persons)(TLB)

What was the purpose of his beating? Isa 53:4-5. "Yet it was our grief he bore, our sorrows that weighed him down. And we thought his troubles were a punishment from God, for his own sins! But he was wounded and bruised for our sins. He was beaten that we might have **peace**; he was lashed— and we were **healed**!" (TLB)

How do we trifle with the death of Christ? If Jesus took every sickness and disease, why do we carry it? We null and void what Jesus was bruised and beaten for.

"That is why many of you are weak and sick, and some have even died."

The death of Christ has two parts to it. One has to do with the beating post experience (**healing / peace**), the second has to do with his dying on the cross. (**salvation**)

111

In this chapter on Consequences, I have listed many examples of how we break our shield of protection, innocently or purposefully. Either way they cause harm that can be avoided just simply by becoming aware that God wants us to live in His presents.

Corrective Measures to Repair the Damage

To repair our shield we must do the same thing David did when he was confronted with his sin, found in <u>Ps. 51:1-19</u>

> [Written after Nathan the prophet had come to inform David of God's judgment against him because of his adultery with Bathsheba, and his murder of Uriah, her husband]. O loving and kind God, have mercy. Have pity upon me and take away the awful stain of my transgressions. Oh, wash me, cleanse me from this guilt. Let me be pure again. For I admit my shameful deed— it haunts me day and night. It is against you and you alone I sinned and did this terrible thing. You saw it all, and your sentence against me is just. Sprinkle me with the cleansing blood and I shall be clean again. Wash me and I shall be whiter than snow. Create in me a new, clean heart, O God, filled with clean thoughts and

right desires. Don't take your Holy Spirit from me. Restore to me again the joy of your salvation, and make me willing to obey you.

Breaking our shield of protection can be stopped because we are the ones in charge, we are the ones who have gone astray. The Lord wants us to get the story straight and receive our full inheritance of peace, prosperity, health and well being for our family. Walking through the veil into His presence brings great rewards.

Chapter # 12

Walking In His Presence

I f we are going to walk in the Lord's presence, we must first know His word that says it is possible. For some people it is as simple as saying - "Oh, Jesus." For others they can't believe He is that close. Jesus left this earth and He is in Heaven, too far away to be approached. In order to experience the presence of Jesus we must walk through the veil of our thinking: Out of the physical and into the spiritual.(Rom. 8:4-9)

Here is a scripture - can you believe it? John 14:18-19 "No, I will not abandon you or leave you as orphans in the storm— I will come to you. In just a little while I will be gone from the world, but I will still be present with you. For I will live again."

If you can believe, "I will still be present with you." then you can talk to the air (physical) or you can talk to Jesus (spiritual).

Can you paint a picture of this Word found in Hebrews 12:22-24? "But you (your name) have come right up into Mount Zion, to the city of the living God, the heavenly Jerusalem, and to the gathering of countless happy angels; and to the church, composed of all those registered in heaven (That's you, if you are born again); and to God who is Judge of all; and to the spirits of the redeemed in heaven, already made perfect (Christians who have died); and to Jesus himself, who has brought us his wonderful new agreement; and to the sprin-kled blood, which graciously forgives instead of crying out for vengeance as the blood of Abel did."

If a person can see (spiritually speaking) this picture then that person can be present with the Lord. Just because he can not see it physically doesn't mean it isn't there.

A person who is born into the Kingdom of God doesn't walk in and out of the kingdom. It is a continual walking in His presence if we would just get it through our thinking.

> Heb 10:19-22 And so, dear brothers, now we
> may walk right into the very Holy of Holies,
> where God is, because of the blood of Jesus.
> This is the fresh, new, life-giving way that
> Christ has opened up for us by tearing the
> curtain— his human body— to let us into the
> holy presence of God. And since this great
> High Priest (Jesus) of ours rules over God's
> household, let us go right in to God himself,

with true hearts fully trusting him to receive
us because we have been sprinkled with
Christ's blood to make us clean and because
our bodies have been washed with pure water.

That experience can happen right now, while a person is
alive. We don't have to wait until we die.

In John 14:22-23 one of Jesus' disciples asked Him,
"Sir, why are you going to reveal yourself only to us disci-
ples and not to the world at large?" Jesus replied, "Because
I will only reveal myself to those who love me and obey me.
The Father will love them too, and we will come to them and
live with them."

Keep in mind we don't live in the world at large, but in
the Kingdom of God. So, there is a constant presences of the
Father, Son and Holy Spirit enveloping us with their love
and protection.

Out of "Pointman Ministries" comes the story of Jim
Ellis who won a medal of honor for taking out a Vietnam
machine gun pocket of resistance. Wanting to commit suicide, he ran up the hill in harm's way of the bullets only to
see them mysteriously deflected. It was years later when he
was having a flash back of the incident that he saw the reason why the bullets didn't hit their target. He saw Jesus in
front of him as the bullets were diverted. He grew up in a
Christian orphanage, but became a rededicated follower
after his experience with Jesus.

Alan Bankhead was in desperate straights, his life in

shambles. During a Singing Christmas Tree program the Spirit of the Lord touched him so, he cried buckets of tears. He came home and immediately feel asleep on the couch, when the Lord walked in and spoke to him. "Give it all to me, Alan." He woke up totally at peace as if a load had been lifted. He gave his life to the Lord Sunday morning at Church, attended the Christmas Tree program in the afternoon, and was delivered in the evening.

A young man walked into a large warehouse and was hit on the head with a metal bar that had fallen ten stories. He was knocked to the ground. Men came to his aid expecting him to be dead. The metal bar was bent in the middle, but he wasn't harmed in any way. He was rushed to the hospital and released - no damage whatsoever. He was a dedicated Christian since Junior High School.

Mavis Mannley, as a young girl, talked to Jesus in the attic of her home out of sight of an abusive father. A neighbor invited her to Church. The first time she ever attended, Jesus sat next to her. She has been a devoted Christian all of her life.

The "Shield of Protection" is available to anyone who wants to walk into His presence.

Works Cited

Aikman, David, "A Tidal Wave of Christianity Sweeps Developing Nations." par. 12, 13, 14. CBN.com. 11 Sept. 2003. <http://cbn.org/cbnnews/cwn/082203 christianity.asp>.

Barton, David, "America to Pray or Not to Pray." 'A statistical look at what has happened since 39 million students stopped praying in public schools.' Brochure 1988.

Buckley, William F., "A Family Cursed?" Book Review. 27, July 2003. par 1-8 <http://news.bbc.co.uk/2/hi/americas/ 2032104.stm>.

CNN, "Episcopal Rev. Gene Robinson""the Diocese of New Hampshire." The Rev. Canon V. Gene Robinso. 'Summary of Experience.' 23 Oct. 2003. <http:// www.nhepiscopal./Bishop.Search/The_Rev_ Canon_V_Gene_Roinson.htm>.

Gola, Stephen. "Divorce Hope" "Can Divorced Christians Remarry? Absolutely." May 2003. Publisher Trafford. Book ISBN 1412000882.

Hulme, Ken. "Saved from the Fire: Family Says Prayers Preserved Home." 20 Nov. 2003 Par. 1,19. <http://www.cbn.com/cbnnews/112103firesurvivor.asp>.

Jenkins, Dr. Phillip. Pen St. Un. Professor of History and Religious Studies. "The Next Christendom: The Coming of Global Christianity."

Loconte, Joseph. "The White House Initiative to Combat AIDS: Leaning from Uganda." 29 Sep 2003.The Heritage Foundation. Par. 1-6. <http:www.heritage.org/Research/ Africa/BG169.cfm>.

McDowell, Josh. "Beyond Belief to Conviction". Video Collection. Josh McDowell Ministries. <www.BeyondBelief.com>.

"PC STUDY BIBLE" version 2.1 For Windows. BibleSoft. 1999. TLB. KJV. NIV.